India's Trade with the ASEAN

A Study on Trends, Determinants and Opportunities

India's Trade with the ASEAN

A Study on Trends, Determinants and Opportunities

Dr. D. Srinivasa Chary
Dr. Radha Raghuramapatruni

ABHIJEET PUBLICATIONS
NEW DELHI 110002

ABHIJEET PUBLICATIONS
4658-A, First Floor, Ambika Bhawan,
21 Ansari Road, New Delhi 110002
Phone: 011-23259444
E-mail: abhijeetpublication@gmail.com
twitter:- @AbhijeetPub21
whatsapp:- 8076785356
instagram: @abhijeet_publications
LinkedIn: jitendra-singh-7729292b/
Website: www.abhijeetpublications.com

INDIA'S TRADE WITH THE ASEAN: A STUDY ON TRENDS, DETERMINANTS AND OPPORTUNITIES

First Published 2021

ISBN 978-93-92816-02-4

PRINTED IN INDIA

Published by J.K. Singh for Abhijeet Publications, New Delhi-110002, Lasertypeset by Abhijeet Typesetters, New Delhi and Printed at Infinity Imaging Systems, New Delhi.

Foreword

It gives me immense pleasure in writing this Foreword to this book authored by Dr. D. Srinivasa Chary & Dr. Radha Raghuramapatruni, rising Indian academicians in the area of International Business. The title they have chosen is important for three reasons: first, when India is celebrating *"Azadi Ka Amrit Mahotsav"*, the country has also completed30 years of its engagement with the Association of South East Asian Nations (ASEAN); and second,India has joined the Indo-Pacific Economic Framework (IPEF), in which many of the ASEAN members are part of; and third, the authors have used an impressive set of tools and models in their analysis to explore India and the ASEAN trade relations.

Independent India was not among the big players of the global trade market till the 1990s. However, following liberalization, India's prowess is being recognized by the world in multiple fronts. India has also intensified its engagements with countries and regions through pragmatic approach and policy framework. The "Look East Policy" was unveiled in order to develop a close relationship with neighboring economies, including especially theSouth-East Asian nations. The "Look East Policy" eventually evolved into "Act East Policy" with a strategic intent since 2014.

India has achieved significant export growth in FY 2022. Nevertheless, modern challenges to the impressive trade performance are not to be ignored. While higher international trade needs to be further promoted, prudent policy steps also have to be taken that achieve internal and external balances. One such policy step involves promotion of free trade agreements in general, and joining the group of nations that willingly accepts free trade as its motto. In case of India, this involves further integration with the Association of South East Asian Nations (ASEAN). In this book Dr. Srinivasachary & Dr. Raghuramapatruni had discussed the issue of Indian economy's trade relations with other 10 -ASEAN countries by using the bi-lateral as well as multi-lateral approach along with detailed analysis of respective economies of the ASEAN. I am impressed by the breadth and the depth of this study. The study uses modern data/models to point out the intricacies of international trade relations as well as political ramifications. The book also uses a vast amount of related literature to point out some interesting facts about India & ASEAN trade. Microeconomic data of specific industries such as information technology are analyzed to further inform the readers about the significance of cooperation with the ASEAN block. Keeping its main focus on India's involvement with the ASEAN block, the book also examines the trade relations, intra-regional trade among the ASEAN, trade intensity, gravity & comparative advantage of the Indian economy with the ASEAN regional group. Lastly, the book sees some prospects for India's comparative advantage in specific sectors like leather, cereals, chemicals, manufactures of base metal, furniture & parts, travel goods, footwear and coffee. In general, it is a magnificent attempt to review the Indian economic performance in the light of ASEAN members' relationship with the Indian polity as well as economy.

Due to the renewed interest in India and the ASEAN relations, with 30 years of their engagement through the "Look East & Act East Policy initiatives" this book is likely to fill the void in literature, and I am sure the policy makers, academia, industry players, opinion makers and students, would find the book an interesting read.

It is quite evident that Dr. Radha Raghuramapatruni is equipped with economic tools to carry out such project. Her research performance until now is extremely impressive. Both the authors had published several research papers in the indexed professional journals, besides sharing their knowledge and experience through presentations in national and international conferences, in the areas of international trade and trade theories. Dr. Radha, whose academic record has been exemplary, has been a regular speaker and consultant for the industries in the area of international trade and expert discussant and editorial writer for many leading media houses. Dr. Srinivasa Chary has huge experience in the area of pharmaceutical exports and manufacturing and I am sure that the readers would find this book of paramount importance and timely addition to their reading list. I wish both the authors all success and due recognition for their contribution.

S. Prahalathan

Chief General Manager
Research & Analysis Group
India Exim Bank, Mumbai

Acknowledgements

With a deep sense of gratitude, I would like to mention about my mentor Dr Radha Raghuramapatruni who was also my supervisor during my Ph.D. My special thanks her for co-authoring this book as well as encouraging me to publish our work. I also thank Sri S. Prahalathan, Chief General Manager–EXIM Bank of India, Mumbai for writing the forward.

I would like to acknowledge here, about my association with GITAM (Deemed to be University) and the erstwhile GITAM School of International Business as a Research Scholar. My sincere thanks to GITAM's authorities and faculty members for equipping me with Research Methodology to explore and study International Business and Trade.

I also would like to mention here the support given by my family members, especially my wife Rekha for her encouragement, sons, and daughter-in-law, for encouraging me continue my academic pursuit. I also thank some of my ex-colleagues and classmates who excelled in academics for inspiring me to undertake academic research, and well wishers who always wished me success.

D. Srinivasa Chary

With a profound sense of respect, I wish to express my deep sense of gratitude to the most respected philanthropist and great visionary, Late Dr. M.V.V.S. Murthi the founder & former President of GITAM (Deemed to be University), Shri. M. Sri Bharat, respected President of GITAM (Deemed to be University), Prof. M. Gangadhara Rao, respected Vice-President, GITAM (Deemed to be University), Shri. M. Bharadwaj, respected Secretary of GITAM (Deemed to be University), Sri Virander Singh Chauhan, honourable Chancellor of GITAM (Deemed to be University), Prof. Dayananda Siddavattam, honourable Vice Chancellor of GITAM (Deemed to be University), Shri Jayasankar E. Variyar respected Pro-Vice Chancellor-Academics of GITAM (Deemed to be University), Shri. D. Gunasekaran, respected Registrar of GITAM (Deemed to be University) and ever grateful to our professional mentor the Dean & Director of GITAM School of Business, Prof. Amit Bhadra for giving us the opportunity and support to bring out our publication.

I also thank Sri S. Prahalathan, Chief General Manager–EXIM Bank of India, Mumbai for writing the forward.

My deep sense of gratitude to my loving grandfather and my teacher, late Shri. R.V.N. Murthy, and grandmother, Smt. R. Lakshmi. My respects to my father late Shri R.N. Rayudu, forever supporting me and giving me the strength to pursue my goals. My sincere thanks to my loving family for their unwavering support in all my academic pursuits. I shall remain obliged to my mentors, friends, colleagues, well-wishers and many good Samaritans who always strongly back me in all my work.

Above all, I am ever thankful to the almighty God for leading me in all my endeavours.

Radha Raghuramapatruni

Contents

List of Tables, Charts and Figures

List of Abbreviations, Acronyms and Symbols

AFTA	ASEAN Free Trade Area
AIFTA	ASEAN-India Free Trade Area
AIJVS	Asian Industrial Joint Ventures
ASEAN	Association of South East Asian Nations
ASSOCHAM	The Associated Chambers of Commerce and Industry of India
CECA	Comprehensive Economic Cooperation
CLMV	Cambodia, Laos, Myanmar and Vietnam countries
FDI	Foreign Direct Investment
FTA	Free Trade Agreement
GATS	General Agreement of Trade in Services
GDP	Gross Domestic Product
HDI	Human Development Index
IMF	International Monetary Fund
NTB	Non-Tariff Barriers
P&C	Parts and Consumables
PTA	Preferential Trade Agreement

RCEP	Regional Comprehensive Economic Partnership
SAARC	South Asian Association for Regional Cooperation
TOI	Trade Openness Indicator
UNCTAD	United Nations Conference on Trade And Development
WTO	World Trade Organization

1

Introduction

> *"The process of globalization is a reality which cannot be denied and should not be avoided. However, it needs to be managed so that we can derive the maximum advantage from world markets."*
>
> *-9th Five Year Plan (1997-2002)*

India had followed protectionist policies during the first few decades after gaining independence in 1947. During the time the private capital was moving to many developed countries, but India was left behind due to in-ward looking economic policies adopted by the government and the resultant sluggish economic growth. The early 1990s saw a change in government policy and the gradual opening of its economy, which was necessitated mainly to subvert the balance of payment crisis. Since then the growth rate has increased from a very low 'Hindu growth rate' to about 6.5% during recent years. The government headed by Mr Narasimha Rao, declared "Look East Policy", as its price motive is to strengthen country's economy through an increase in trade with Asian countries as the later economies were booming and it provided India with fresh opportunities to look into which were not utilised until then. India, now, is among major world economies having potential in trade with the right basket of imports and exports covering traditional and non-traditional goods.

1.1 INDIA'S CHANGING PATTERN OF THE WORLD TRADE

When British were ruling India, export surplus registered in foreign trade in India through exports of raw materials and plantation-based crops. However, the surplus in exports was not considered as economic gains for India because the surplus was used to import consumer products and funds were transferred back to Britain. Thus, India's foreign trade was systematically being exploited by British rulers. Textiles were among the top imports while cotton was accounted for a substantial share in exports of India.

Post-world war II, there was a revival in the pattern of world trade, especially after India's independence until the 1980s. Reduction in transportation costs and reconstruction of economies also helped industrialized nations to revive the world trade through the initiatives such as "GATT (General Agreement on Tariff and Trade)" that reduced barriers to the International business. Late 1950's witnessed adaptation of convertibility of currency by major industrialized countries on current accounts, and it has facilitated further expansion of international trade. Several developing countries also started to open up their economies during the 1980s through 1990s, and some of the Asian countries also have started to expand their foreign trade by participating in the world economy. The strategies adopted by countries towards an open economy during this time were based on efficient allocation of resources, emphasis on modern technologies, deriving benefits from scale. Unlike its Asian counterparts, India could not derive the benefits of increased openness in international trade. However, the government had introduced the Exim Policy in 1985 for three years to focus on international trade. However, initially, the trade was characterized by high tariff levels and licensing system, which lead to the isolation of the country's economy from the rest. India's government policies with regards to Industrial and foreign investment were also restricting the investments in Foreign trade. In this backdrop, the Indian Government has brought in economic reforms in 1991, that helped liberalization along with the opening of India to the world trade.

1.2 THE 1991 ECONOMIC POLICY REFORMS

Despite the excellent high performance during the seventh five-year plan (1985-90), due to the number of factors, such as reduced internal production in oil and petroleum, the gains in invisible accounts have reduced and brought down with it opportunities for foreign assistance. Debt service obligations also increased, and payments to external lenders also have become critical. By 1991-92, despite the reduction in prices of oil in world markets, the balance of payment had become worse. To counter this, the Government of India had taken two concrete steps. First one was to seek assistance from the international financial institutions for obtaining immediate relief. The second one was to initiate economic reforms, especially for trade and exchange rate policy by resorting to rupee depreciation to increase the competitiveness of the Indian economy. There were deliberate concrete efforts made through policy reforms of 1991 to blend the Indian economy with the world economy. This new policy of exchange rate and trade regime targeted the elimination of unwanted administrative and discretionary controls on foreign trade in order to make India more competitive. The exchange rate adjustments and the policy promulgated greatly lessened import controls and facilitated exports through a favourable exchange rate. Licensing restrictions could not be removed although they were slightly reduced.

In the interim, a few activities were taken for advancement in exports. The Exim Policy revised the current approach to give a higher surplus to agricultural exports and labour-intensive goods in which India enjoys a comparative advantage. Negative list of products from the export basket was significantly cut off. Fiscal and financial policy reforms were also taken to support export efforts. The government reduced the duties on imports of capital goods required for clothing articles, leather, marine items, gems and jewellery, processed food, and horticulture. The foreign currency packing credit was considerably made flexible, making the loans available to exporters at globally competitive interest rates. In short, India's government indicated that the policy initiative to liberalize and globalize the economy was a trans-national arrangement from inward-looking trade policy to an open one. The initiatives of the country through the 1991 economic policy reforms and the structural and fiscal initiatives surely paid off the country as today the country could get its place among the major players in terms of growth rate and development.

1.3 INDIA'S JOURNEY FROM "LOOK EAST POLICY" TO "ACT EAST POLICY"

India was not among big players of the global trade market up to the 1990s. India commenced the "Look East Policy (LEP)" initiative in 1991, trying to gain better access to the regional markets in Asia. India always needed to develop a close relationship with neighboring economies, including South-East Asia. As India got independence, Prime Minister Jawaharlal Nehru said that 'India is the gateway to both West and South-East Asia.'. In Nehru's opinion, close relation with East is vital due to India's geographical proximity with Eastern countries, shared a cultural ethos, similar historical past, and shared economic and strategic goals. The India-South East Asia relations have suffered due to India's defeat to China during the war in 1962. Foreign policymakers of Indian also have neglected the region during the period. This resulted in India's closeness with the Soviet block and a Friendship Treaty with it in the year 1971. As the cold war ended, it brought in the onset of the policy changes during the 1991s, which lead to reorientation of the India and South–East Asia relations. Few significant events took place around 1991, including disintegration of USSR, termination of cold war and Crisis of Balance of Payments in India. The Indian Government had tackled the balance of payments crisis through liberalization of the economy. Liberalization reforms including 'Look East Policy' promulgated during 1991. India wanted to bring back the attention towards its neighborhood that got diluted during the cold war era. The 'Look East Policy' signified importance of East Asia as an excellent opportunity for trade, new areas for business, and stimulation for economic development and growth.

The "Look East Policy" pursues four objectives. The first objective was to reform and liberalize the Indian economy and accelerate closer trade association with South-East Asian countries. The liberalization and economic reforms introduced in association with "Look Easy Policy" were to reduce trade barriers and motivate investments. Further, India's zeal for Free Trade Agreements created a new dynamism into its 'Look East Policy' which positively impacted trade reforms and liberalization. The second objective was to sustain the increased pace of growth. It was essential for India to engage with East Asia and tap into later's growth. India believes that trading with East Asia is crucial in order to sustain its economic growth. Stable trade relations with countries in East Asia would enable India to gain access to the growth possibilities with Asia. The third objective is the promotion of economic regionalism in East Asia. This initiative was also due to the influence of the formation of such trade blocs in other parts of the world, such as Europe and North America. The fourth objective of the policy is it could be instrumental in addressing the inequalities in development in India and in fostering more equitable growth because north-eastern states (Manipur, Arunachal Pradesh, Meghalaya, Tripura, Mizoram and Nagaland) are lagging in development when compared to the remaining states in the country. India aimed at linking up the North-Eastern states with South-East Asia peninsula and initiate economic development and through the development of better logistics, improved infrastructure, Trade, agri-business, investment, and other trade activities. Geographically, India's north-eastern states have a common border with Indonesia and Thailand by sea, and with Myanmar by land.

The primary reason for the push and to a significant extent, the accomplishment of "Look East Policy" was India's close cultural and geographic proximity to the Asian countries. India and South-East Asia had more than a thousand years of trade relationships in the past, which influenced each other in terms of cultural, religious, linguistic and business aspects. South-East Asia has also been the major haven for the Indian migrants. The 'Look East Policy' presented a potential role in addressing the gap between Asian countries and India. When India got reunited with the countries in Southeast Asia, India found, to its surprise, that the region has progressed significantly into a prosperous region compared to what it was in the 1940s and 50s. India also has strategic intent in engaging with South East Asia. During the early 2000s, India was concerned about the growing protectionist policies in Europe and the USA, and if the negotiations with WTO failed, India would have to face the consequences on its own. Although India started signing trade agreements with several countries to have many options at its disposal, the engagement with East Asian countries has a special place as the most energetic and potential trade partners.

Within the 10-15 years, the 'Look East Policy' has gone beyond mere trade objectives of aligning with South East Asia's growth. The policy today covers broader aspects as the economy continues the growth path. Although initially, the importance was to improve India's trade with ASEAN, and other countries such as Korea and Japan. Subsequently, this engagement has attained a broader scope, including political, social, cultural, and security-related aspects as well. Especially in the light of increasing domination of China in Asia, India needed to consolidate its position in the neighborhood to counter this and bring a balance of power for protecting its interests. Today, India and ASEAN relations have traversed a long, journey with several achievements to reach the year 2017, and the partnership has completed 25 years of partnership. India and the ASEAN recognise each other's role in the development of the region and shaping its future. Towards this objective, the "Look East' Policy" of India had transformed into "Act East Policy" in 2014. Today, ASEAN-India put together to consist of a vast economic entity with an approximate population of 180 crores, total Gross Domestic Product (GDP) of greater than 3 trillion US dollars. Despite an impressive trajectory of trade history between two nations, there is further scope for growth by the integration of India into the production value chains of ASEAN. The Asia-Pacific is among the world's dynamic regions today, and both India and ASEAN must play a vital role in shaping the so-called 'Asian Century.' Before analysing trade relations of India with ASEAN and its member countries, it would be fit of the hour to under the formation and perspective at the bottom of emergence of the ASEAN regional group and its journey.

1.4 "THE ASSOCIATION OF SOUTH-EAST ASIAN NATIONS"

"The Association of South-East Asian Nations (ASEAN) was formed in 1967" (asean.org) initially with Malaysia, Singapore, Philippines, Thailand and Indonesia. Initially, it was ASEAN-5, Brunei joined the group in the year 1984 after attaining independence from the UK, Vietnam joined the group in the year 1955, Myanmar and Laos in the year 1997, and Cambodia joined in the year 1999 thus the current membership of ASEAN is ten. Since the beginning, ASEAN was regarded as a successful regional trade block among developing regions of the world. It has also been responsible for continuing stability and peace in South-East Asia for more than forty years. Before the ASEAN was formed, there were many conflicts among the South-East Asian members. However, finally, the countries found them unproductive and cleared the way to form ASEAN as a regional body to balance the inter-country relations so that resources which could be free to be used for building unified states which were divided into ethnic, cultural religious lines. A decade later of the formation of the ASEAN in 1976, ASEAN's first treaty articulated formally. "The treaty of Amity and Co-operation in South-East Asia (TAC)," (asean.org) has framed the basic principles for maintaining the relations among the member states. The Treaty had modest goals which were limited to moderating the relations between the member states. The association then had taken up other avenues of cooperation especially those related to the environment, trade liberalization, a multitude of security-related problems which include transnational crime, for example, piracy of ships, drug trafficking and other development-related problems such as poverty and development of rural areas.

During mid1990s, ASEAN regional group could not offer a reasonable explanation to some of the criticism that it has faced, for example, pollution coming from forest fires of Indonesia, human rights problem in Myanmar and the financial crisis in 1997-98. Many international business firms also criticized the group for not acting against the policies of trade protectionism. In 2003, ASEAN took an oath to promote an ASEAN Community by 2020, in south-East Asia, by co-operating in the three mutually reinforcing areas which are politics, security, economic, and socio-cultural realm. Consequently, the ASEAN community would have the three active components, "the ASEAN Security Community, ASEAN Economic Community and ASEAN Socio-Cultural Community" (asean.org). ASEAN countries have developed a Charter to turn the ASEAN to a rule-based organization. The regional group behind the resolutions aimed to make ASEAN play a role as community security, promoting political and social stability during the unstable times.

Along with this, the disintegration of the USSR left the ASEAN for a new order to manage security; ASEAN has incorporated the following forums for addressing regional challenges in recent times.

"ASEAN Free Trade Area (AFTA)"

When the ASEAN formed "ASEAN Free Trade Area (AFTA)" (asean.org) during the year 1992 (that would eventually become a free trade zone over 15 years). Southeast Asia's Leaders were not expecting the expansion of intra-regional trade. Instead, they hope that the region would attract investors from all over the world as it is a single economic and geographical space. Economic growth was the main factor that defines political validity between the ASEAN countries and a vital tool in which respective governmental authorities become strong politically and manage social and political stability in the different societies. The formation of AFTA was intended to get an inflow of Foreign Direct Investment into the member countries. Finally, the first phase of ASEAN concluded successfully in the year 2002, ahead of the scheduled time.

"ASEAN Regional Forum (ARF)"

"The ASEAN regional forum" (asean.org) was launched in the year 1993, and its objective was to promote security in the region of Asia-Pacific. The group's contribution to the cause involved more of a discussion than a coordinated action. Still, white papers, the military exchange programs, and the formation of experts who are available to mediate during the conflicts have led to more transparency and increased defence cooperation.

"ASEAN Plus Three (APT) Cooperation"

"ASEAN Plus Three Cooperation" (asean.org) was started in the year 1997. APT intends to increase the collaboration among ASEAN, Japan, South Korea and China and considered as very logical and crucial Asian formation.

East-Asia Summit:

East-Asia Summit held in 2005 for the first time. The objective of the summit was to strengthen security and promote development in East Asia, and it was attended by representative heads from Asian countries such as India, Australia, New Zealand, South Korea, China, Japan and member states of ASEAN. During the past decade, China took an aggressive track in border disputes with India, Sovereignty in the Sea, and the Mekong River. Many contemporary scholars have warned that some of the countries, including Vietnam and Malaysia, are trying to protect their strategic interests and energy resources in the South-China Sea. Investments in the arms purchase in South-East Asia have increased twice between the years

2005 and the year 2009. Though ASEAN's engagement with the world is rising, experts have opined that considerable hurdles to multilateral co-operation remain. The ASEAN countries' policy does not promote interference in member affairs; hence, the foreign policy of each country is shaped by a state-centric approach and undermine the regional integration initiatives.

ASEAN Plus six (APS)

The regional framework of "ASEAN plus six", with the ten members of ASEAN and India, Japan, China, New Zealand, South Korea and Australia was formed at the 1st "East Asian Summit" during 2005. Earlier the grouping was called "ASEAN plus Three" (The ASEAN plus South Korea, Japan and China) which tried to develop regional cooperation and to focus on problems and issues, for example, Asian currency issue that broke out during the year 1997. The ASEAN+6 framework produced a group with countries presenting bigger market and more resource base by adjoining Australia, India and New Zealand to ASEAN +3. The formation of ASEAN+6 was partly due to the initiative taken by India with its vast population and high growth expectations. India has been living with many problems such as lack of infrastructure, which are very important for economic growth. India started economic reforms around the year 1991, but in comparison East Asian countries, it has not been able to integrate into the global economy fully, and it still has internal regulations and trade barriers with other countries.

ASEAN is becoming a significant economic powerhouse in the South-East Asian region, which has signed FTA's with China, Australia, India, Korea, Japan and India. ASEAN and the USA have "Trade and Investment Framework Agreement (TIFA)" (csis.org), but it was not sufficient. Japan was a significant trading partner of ASEAN till the year 2009, but China surpassed Japan since the year 2010 to contribute to 11 % of the ASEAN's international trade, increasing by 21% to $280 billion in the year 2011. The second-largest trade block of ASEN is European Union (EU), and the first one is China, comprising 11 % of the total trade. India –ASEAN trade is also growing at great heights, both the countries put together to consist of one among the prominent economic and geographical entities having a population of 180 crores and a GDP of about 3 trillion US dollars. ASEAN is India's 4th most significant trade partner, and it accounts for 10.2 % of total trade of India. Although an impressive trajectory of trade relations between the nations, Diversity among member states of ASEAN has caused difficulties in the removal of trade barriers, the FTAs which were implemented in the recent times may not be able to tackle the problems caused by institutional obstacles to the trade, because the legal framework required to implement the FTAs was not fully developed. The low level of governance and not so reliable judicial systems in the ASEAN also caused obstacles to trade as it leads to difficulties in enforcing contracts. ASEAN has been facing some challenges, including disputes among member states over sovereignty in the South-China Sea. According to some of the experts, the ASEAN group suffers from a cohesive diplomatic effort due to the differences in priorities of the member nations and the inability of the leadership to address the same. Thus, ASEAN was prevented from making meaningful progress in negotiations and resolutions to many problems.

1.5 EVOLUTION OF INDIA-ASEAN RELATIONS OVERTIME

India had renewed engagements with South-East Asia during the early 1990s, and the cooperation between India and ASEAN has steadily improved. The aftermath of the cold war, as well as an increase in prominence of the

Asian region, also allowed India to explore close cooperation with ASEAN. India has initiated actions to gradually improve relations that could promise economic possibilities which could further enhance India's political and diplomatic relations. During the year March 1992, India has been given a status of "sectoral dialogue partner" to the ASEAN group, that enabled India to participate in the exchange of specific areas like trade, investment, and tourism. During 1995, the India and ASEAN relations had dramatically taken upward turn when India was given the status of a "full dialogue partner" with the ASEAN and allowed to make its appearances in "ARF" and the "Post-Ministerial Conference (PMC)" meeting. Towards the end of cold war, the interests of both India and ASEAN have come together with regards to security aspects as well as economic interests, which were guided by India's "Look Easy policy". ASEAN too has shown immense interest in India's alliance as India was never considered a political or security threat.

In order to increase its international trade, India needed to integrate with the world economies, and East-Asian countries have been considered as a high trajectory because of their economic progress and development. While India's trade volume with the ASEAN had improved positively since the year 1991, the pattern of trade has been inconsistent through the region with individual countries. It could be due to differences in complementarities among the different countries' economies of the ASEAN with India, and differences in tariff levels. Trade with Singapore was a major contributor to the trade between India and ASEAN. Trade with Indonesia and Malaysia is slowing catching the pace, Thailand, and the Philippines are becoming unexpectedly impressive.

The rest of ASEAN -5, countries like Brunei and Laos PDR are hardly taking advantage of India-ASEAN collaboration in any form of trade. In the economies of

Singapore, Malaysia and Thailand, shortage of labour resources for the workforce in many sectors has made India as a major source of skilled labour to these countries. While the skilled Indian workforce has migrated to South-East Asian countries, India opened up as an essential destination with trade potential, networks of communication, and availability of a skilled workforce at a reasonable price.

Trade partnership between ASEAN and India was initiated in a positive direction after the year 1991 but has taken time to take off. The potential investors of the ASEAN followed a wait and saw attitude towards India because of the fears regarding the uncertainties concerning the stability of government, fluid political environment, and unforeseeable recall of foreign investments in India. The fears of protectionism, corruption, bureaucratic hindrances, power storage, lack of clear policy initiatives dampened the initial enthusiasm of collaboration between the ASEAN and India and raised doubts about the potential from associating with India. Singapore is the country to take the first step in the integration of its economy with India as it believes that its integration with the Indian economy would enhance the development of both the nation and will contribute to a more stable environment. Furthermore, Singapore saw the potential in associating with India for developing its tourism and software industry. Later, the other countries of the ASEAN also understood the importance of engaging with India as it would help stabilize the region and counter the influence of Japan and China. So, Singapore worked as a catalyst between ASEAN countries and India to initiate the ties and the process of strong trade, political and institutional integration between the two regions. The fruits of these ties were very impressive not just in terms of economic relations but extended to the cultural and social terms too, which would further impact the trade relations positively. After India became "sectoral dialogue partner" to ASEAN, it is quite evident that trade volumes of India with ASEAN increased, compared with other countries. From 1993 to 2003, India-ASEAN bilateral trade had grown at a rate of 11. 2 % per annum from US$ 2.9 billion in 1993 to 12.1 billion in 2003. Both regions realized the scope for increasing the trade between them and started negotiating on a plan document to create "ASEAN-India Free Trade Area". India's "Look East Policy" good response from several ASEAN countries with similar interests for expanding their business interests westward. India and ASEAN have signed "ASEAN-India Framework Agreement on Comprehensive Economic Co-operation" at "2nd ASEAN-India Summit on 8th October 2003 in Bali, Indonesia" (asean.org). This framework of this agreement prepared the groundwork for starting an "ASEAN-India regional trade and investment area (RTIS)" eventually, which concludes Free Trade Agreement which covers not only goods but also services and investments. This was followed by "ASEAN-India Trade in Goods Agreement", August 2009 and the "ASEAN-India Free Trade Agreement (AIFTA)", January 2010. The "7th ASEAN-India Summit" in Bangkok on October 24th, 2009 decided to amend the targets for bilateral trade to US$ 70 billion in the next two years. ASEAN-India trade has grown more than 22 % per year during the period 2005 to 2011 period. India and the ASEAN trade increased by greater than 37% in 2011-12, up to US$ 79 billion, exceeding the target set in the year 2009. India and ASEAN have concluded the negotiation on FTA in the year 2002 during the "10th ASEAN-India Summit" in Delhi. Both the partners expect the two way trade between them to rise to $ 200 billion by the year 2025. Both the regions were also working towards enhancement of private sector participation from both sides through "reactivation of the ASEAN-India Business Council (AIBC), the holding of the first ASEAN-India Business Summit (AIBS) and an ASEAN-India

Business Fair (AIBF)" (AINTT Proceedings, 2012) The "ASEAN Transport Ministers (ATM)" gathering in the Philippines during November 2008, has concluded the "ASEAN-India aviation cooperation framework" for cooperation in aviation sectors of India and the ASEAN. The "2nd meeting of the Tourism ministers of India and ASEAN" was held on 2010 January 25th, firmly acknowledged India's proposal for establishing "ASEAN-India Tourism Working Group". Participants of the meeting have backed the proposal to establish an "ASEAN promotional chapter for tourism" in Mumbai as a stage for "ASEAN National Tourism Organization (NTO)" to promote South-East Asia to the people in India and to bring awareness among ASEAN countries and India. "ASEAN-India TIG agreement" enabled the establishment of one among prominent FTAs in the world, which can create a market of around 180 crore population and a combined Gross Domestic Product of 3 trillion US dollars. The India-ASEAN Trade agreement has come into effect, including all countries of ASEAN except Indonesia. Since January 2010, as per the AIFTA, the tariff liberalization would eventually apply to 75% of the trade between the partner countries. The FTA is aimed at the removal of tariffs on 4,000 products such as machinery, electronics, textiles and chemicals. Out of these products, by 2013, import duties will be reduced on 3,200 products, and balance 800 products were to be reduced to nil duty by 2016. Most of the international trade of India with ASEAN is concentrated into Thailand, Indonesia, Malaysia and Singapore. In pursuit of the objective to accelerate the trade the regional group, India's "Look East Policy" was followed by "Act East Policy" during 2014. India hosted "ASEAN-India Commemorative Summit" in New Delhi on the occasion of Republic Day 26th January 2018 for completion of 25 years of its Look East Policy. ASEAN-India trade increased by nearly 14% during 2017-18 to 81.3 billion US dollars. Imports and exports of India from and to ASEAN were 47.13 billion US dollars and 34.2 billion US dollars respectively.

1.6 IMPORTANCE AND SCOPE OF STUDY

The growth in India's economy is the result of the deliberate changes in its approach to economic policy, especially after the 1991 macro-economic crisis. The country has moved from 'inward-looking strategy' to an 'outward-looking strategy' and the initiative of its 'Look East Policy' has a significant bearing on the integration of its domestics economy with the external world especially the East Asian countries which had resulted in sizeable outcome thereby increasing its trade volumes. ASEAN also recognizes India as a growing power in Asia and interested in engaging with India that could be helpful to ASEAN countries. ASEAN too can benefit from India's development in science and technology, service and the economic sector. ASEAN looks towards developing an all-round economic relation with India. India also understands that ASEAN countries have made significant progress in the last twenty years, and it can gain from the partners' current status of economic development. It is also essential for India, to take advantage of the strategic location of ASEAN for its stability and economic security.

The establishment of the regional grouping SAARC was not successful. The slow growth, the disintegration of USSR also has resulted in the need to find new partners for India. Hence India's proclamation of "Look-East Policy" during 1992 began the course of revitalizing its trade relationship with the ASEAN member nations. "Look-East Policy" has seen India attempting to increase economic relations with some of the ASEAN countries, especially with India was designated as "sectoral dialogue partner" to. ASEAN. The India-ASEAN two-way trade has tripled, and the future was promising. Currently, the cooperation between the partners is not just restricted to trade alone but also encompassed several other fields. Today, India and ASEAN relations have passed through a dynamic journey with several achievements to reach the year 2017, and the two regions have completed 25 years of partnership. In order to realize this objective, the "Look East" Policy had morphed into "Act East Policy" by 2014.

Today, the ASEAN-India together form a prominent economic grouping. ASEAN occupies 4th largest position in India's trade, comprising of 10.2% of India's total trade. India occupies 7th position in the trade of ASEAN, and there are perfect complementarities between service economy of India and manufacturing-oriented ASEAN. Despite an impressive trajectory of economic relations between the two nations, still, there is enough room for expanding the trade relations through India's integration into the value chains of ASEAN. Asia-Pacific region is among the most progressive regions of the globe today, and both ASEAN and India must play a central role in shaping the so-called 'Asian Century.' Considering such turn of events, the study intends to explore the intensity of India-ASEAN trade relations and study about different factors impacting the trade. Further, the study assesses the commodity trade patterns between India and ASEAN and analyzes promising commodity categories for increasing trade in future and analyzes in detail the "Intra Industry Trade" among identified commodity product groups for India and the ASEAN.

1.7 OBJECTIVES OF THE STUDY

- To study the bilateral trade pattern between India and the ASEAN regional group under the study period 2000 to 2017.

- To examine the intensity of trade relations between India and the ASEAN countries during the period.
- To assess the potential of commodity trade pattern between India and the ASEAN region and find the commodity categories with future trade potentiality.
- To analyze the extent of "Intra industry trade" for the various commodity groups taken for the study of India and the ASEAN group and identify the direction of the trade pattern of these commodities.
- To identify the factors affecting the trade between India and the ASEAN regional group.
- To assess trade prospects between India and ASEAN from emerging opportunities.

1.8 HYPOTHESES

Ho: India's trade share with the ASEAN group has continuously been on the rise, and this has gained momentum during the last decade.

H1: India's trade share with the ASEAN group has not been on the rise during the last decade.

Ho: There is a difference in the composition of trade between India and the ASEAN during the study period

H1: There is no difference in the composition of trade between India and the ASEAN during the study period.

Ho: There is a change in the pattern of commodity trade between India and the ASEAN.

H1: There is no change in the pattern of commodity trade between India and the ASEAN.

Ho: There are an immense scope and prospects for future trade between India and the ASEAN

H1: There are no scope and prospects for future trade between India and the ASEAN

1.9 SOURCE OF DATA

The study uses secondary data, collected from sources including UN Publications, IMF publications, and Publications of World Bank. UN Publications include "United Nations Statistical Year Book", Foreign Trade Statistics, "Statistical Yearbook of Asia and the Pacific", "International Trade Statistics", "UNCTAD Handbook of International Trade and Development", Statistical Papers of Commodity Trade Statistics, Human Development Report and World Investment Directory for Asia and the Pacific. The IMF Publications, including "The Direction of Trade Statistics(DOTS)", "International Financial Statistics", have been used. "World Bank publications" such as the World Development Report, Asian Development Outlook have also been extensively used.

1.10 METHODOLOGY

In general, the study period covers the years 2000 to 2017, except in a few chapters where availability of the data for the period is restricted., to study the trends 15 years is considered to make meaningful analyses and also to explore prospects of bilateral trade for the future. The following indices and models were used in the analysis of the Trends and Prospects of Bilateral Trade between India and ASEAN. Some of these indices have been used extensively in earlier studies of bilateral trade between different regions as well as some specific analyses in research studies on India and ASEAN.

1.10.1 Intensity Indices

"Trade Intensity Index" has two components. "Export-Intensity Index (XII)" and "Import- Intensity Index (MII)" have been used for observing the pattern of exports and imports. Following A.J. Brown (1947) they can be defined as follows:

Export- intensity index

"The ratio of the export share of a country/region to the share of world exports going to a partner. Export - Intensity Index (XII) can be defined as,

$$XII_{ij} = \frac{x_{ij}/X_{iw}}{x_{wj}/X_{ww}}$$

Where x_{ij} is the value of total exports of country/region i to country/region j, X_{iw} is the value of the total exports of country/region i to the world, x_{wj} is the value of total world exports to country/region j, and X_{ww} is the value of total world exports. An XII of greater than one indicates that trade flow between countries/regions is larger than expected, given their importance in world trade" (A.J. Brown, 1947)

Import- Intensity index:

"The ratio of import share of a country/region to the share of world imports going to a partner Import -Intensity Index (MII) can be defined as,

$$MII_{ij} = M_{ij} / M_{iw} / M_{wj} / M_{ww}$$

Where M_{ij} is the dollar value of imports of country/region i to country/region j, M_{iw} is the dollar value of the imports of country/region i to the world, M_{wj} is the dollar value of world imports to country/region j, and M_{ww} is the dollar value of world imports. An index of greater than one indicates that there is a higher import intensity between the countries." (A.J. Brown, 1947)

Additionally, to assess the degree of trade relations that occur between nations and analyze the background as per the study, the export and import trade shares of bilateral trade between "India and ASEAN" and growth rates about them are defined as follows.

Trade shares

"It is the percentage of trade with a partner to total trade of a country/region. It is computed as the dollar value of total trade of country/region i with country/region j expressed as a percentage share of the dollar value of total trade of country/region i with the world. A higher share indicates a higher degree of integration between partner countries/regions" (Nassir Ul Haq Wani, February 2013). The trade share of exports and imports of India concerning ASEAN was calculated for analysis.

Growth Rates

The growth rate is the rate of change, and it is calculated as the difference between the corresponding period in the current year and previous year for a frequency of the data (a month or quarter). It can be expressed as follows:

"(Value in the current year – Value in Previous year) / Value in Previous year * 100."

The exports and import growth rates of India with ASEAN countries were calculated from the year 1990 to 2010.

1.10.2 Revealed Comparative Advantage Index (RCA)

RCA was used as a gold standard in trade theory, which was propounded by Balassa in 1965. The RCA is used to indicate trade potential in specific commodities/segment of commodities a country has compared to total exports of the country, in relation to the total exports of that commodity/ segment of commodities in the world and is expressed using following equation.

"B or RCA $_{ij}$= $(X_{ij}/ X_{it})/ (X_{wj}/X_{wt})$

Where X_{ij} is the Country's exports of product j, X_{it} is the country's total exports; X_{wt} is the World's total exports of product j, X_{wt} is the entire world's exports. A value of more than 1 implies the country has 'revealed comparative advantage' in the product and a value of less than 1 implies revealed comparative disadvantage in the product." By examining the RCA of different trade partners in different commodities/segments, we can identify trade potential between those partner countries. If RCA between two trade partners in a given product/segment is similar, it denotes limited trade potential between those partners in the given product/ segment, unless there is "Intra Industry Trade" in that product/segment is present.

Volrath's Revealed Competitiveness Index:

Volrath advised an extended version of RCA which is known as Revealed Competitiveness and expressed by the following equation

RC or RTA = RXA - RMA

Where RC is "Revealed Competitiveness (and RTA is Related Trade Advantage) is the difference between Relative Export Advantage (RXA) and Relative Import Advantage (RMA) of country i in product or segment j." Eiteljorge and Hartmann used this.

"RC= In RXA-In RMA".

Volrath also used the above indices in logarithmic form as it has the advantage of being symmetric through the origin, and this equation is expressed by

RC - In RCA - In RMA

If all the above three indices, i.e., RCA, RTA, and RC, are positive, it denotes comparative /competitive advantage for the given country in the product/segment.

1.10.4 The Lafay's Index:

Lafay's index presents trade specialization of a country for a commodity/service as the "difference between the trade balance of that good/service and the country's overall trade balance, weighted by the good's share of total trade." (Alessandrini, Michele, 2011) Lafay's index captures trade flows in terms of "Intra Industry Trade", that is common to many industry segments. The advantage in using "Lafay's revealed comparative advantage index" (LFI hereafter) is, it can deal with "distortions due to the macroeconomic fluctuations" (Lafay, 1992). In essence, each product's contribution is weighted by the LFI as per its importance in trade. The following is the Lafay's index used in the analysis:

$$LFI^i_j = 100\left(\frac{x^i_j - m^i_j}{x^i_j + m^i_j} - \frac{\sum_{j=1}^{N}\left(x^i_j - m^i_j\right)}{\sum_{j=1}^{N}\left(x^i_j + m^i_j\right)}\right)\frac{x^i_j + m^i_j}{\sum_{j=1}^{N}\left(x^i_j - m^i_j\right)}$$

where "LF^i_j: Lafay index of product j in country i. , xj: Exports of product j towards the rest of the world, mj: Imports of product j from the rest of the world.

N: Number of traded goods. As per this index, the country's comparative advantage in product j is calculated as the difference between product j normalized trade balance and overall normalized trade balance." (Lafay, 1992)

Hence, LFI values for the product j for any year should add up to zero. Since LFI gives a product's "contribution to the overall country's normalized trade balance", we can deduct that if LFI value for product j is positive, it indicates a comparative advantage in product j. Similarly, if the LFI value for product j is higher, that means there is greater specialization, and that specific product/product group's contribution is more significant in the overall trade balance, If LFI is negative, it means that the product/ product group is relying on imports.

1.10.5 Intra Industry Trade Index

As discussed earlier, "Intra industry trade" between partners in a given commodity can negate the results of the RCA, that means, the two-way trade between the countries is possible for future growth in a given commodity/segment if there is a significant "Intra industry trade" despite similar RCA profiles between the two trade partners.

Grubel and Lloyd's index (GL Index) has been used in the literature before to measure the trade intensity in the same commodity group/ industry between two countries, the formula used to measure the GL index is given below.

"$IIT_{jt} = (X_{jt} + M_{jt})$"$X_{jt} + M_{jt}\ (X_{jt} + M_{jt}))$

where: X_{jt} = value of exports from India to ASEAN in industry j and year t, M_{jt}= value of imports to India from ASEAN in industry j and year t" (Grubel, H., & Lloyd, P. 1975)

"IIT_{jt}" is used to measure the extent of integration in the industry j, and the weighted average of its trade is taken to calculate IIT among a group of commodities or manufacturing sector as a whole.

HIIT refers to "Horizontal Intra industry trade", and it takes place when the traded products are of same quality or stage of processing, whereas VIIT refers to "Vertical Intra Industry Trade" where goods the quality of goods differs, or they are derived from different process stage. According to the standard research practice, unit values of similar products of export versus import are within a range of 0.75 to 1.25 is considered as HIIT, and those which are outside this range are considered VIIT.

1.10.6 Gravity Model Specification

The data for calculation of the gravity model has been taken from bilateral trade and other indices between India and the ASEAN regional grouping for a period of 25 years from 1991 to 2016.

For analysis, balance panel data, which consists of 6600 two-way trade data points spanning different variables related to the gravity model, has been processed. Two different types of augmented gravity model have been used in the study. Different "Panel Data Estimation Techniques" was employed to determine a model which is more suitable to give the desired results. These techniques include "Pooled OLS method (POLS)", "Maximum likelihood Estimation Method (MLE)", "Fixed Effect with Vector Decomposition (FEVD)", "Between Effect (BE)" and "Random Effect Method (RE)".

Two types of "augmented gravity model" are employed in the study. The first model has GDP along with other traditional variables as determinant variables and bilateral trade between India and ASEAN as an independent variable. The formula used in the model (*as given by* B.P. Sarath Chandran, 2018) is given below.

$$"\ln(TT_{ij}) = \alpha + \beta_1 \ln GDP_i + \beta_2 \ln GDP_j + \beta_3 \ln PCGDP_i + \beta_4 \ln PCGDP_j + \beta_5 \ln PCGDP_{diff}$$

$$-\beta_6 \ln Distance +$$

$$\beta_7 ASEANmember - \beta_8 ContBord - \beta_9 ComLang - \beta_{10} ComColony + \varepsilon_{ij}"$$

Here,

"Ln (TT)ij = Log of Total trade between country i and j for a year

Ln GDPi = log of GDP of country i

Ln GDPj = log of GDP of country j

Ln PCGDPi = log of per capita income of country i

Ln PCGDPj = log of per capita income of country j

Ln PCGDP diff = absolute difference in per capita of country i and j

Ln Distance = log of geographical distance between country i and j

ASEAN member = dummy representing common membership to ASEAN FTA

Cont Border = dummy if countries share common border

Com Lang = dummy if countries share common official language

Com Colony = dummy if both countries were under the same colonizer

εij = Error term"

2

Review of Literature

This chapter aims to review the literature about the trade relations between "India and ASEAN" and the concepts used in the methodology adopted for the study. Thus, the literature survey is presented in five sections. The first section has references to the theories of trade which provide basis and rationale for international trade as well as explain how the division of labour and endowments can contribute to welfare and growth of the nations concerned. In this section, There are also references to the writings establishing tools and indices such as Gravity index, RCA (Revealed Comparative Advantage), GL index etc. which help understand the natural drivers of the growth in international trade. The second section has references to the studies done by various authors about Look East policy and the international trade between India & ASEAN. The third section has references to the studies about concerns and issues in India and ASEAN bilateral trade, the fourth section presents the summary, and the fifth section mentions gaps in the literature.

2.1 THEORIES OF INTERNATIONAL TRADE

As stated by "Van den Berg and Lewer (2007)", Adam Smith stated that "increasing specialization and the division of labour, coupled with international exchange, would contribute to raising welfare and growth of a nation". For Smith, "International trade has a very positive effect on economic growth. A sudden shift in trade policy that opens up new trade provides an immediate gain in real per capita income, which, in turn, accelerates technological progress and increases the rate of economic growth" (Van den Berg and Lewer, 2007).

As stated by Steven M. Suronovic (2009) David Ricardo stated that when two countries engage in trade, "despite differences in terms of technology or wages, would lead to a 'win-win' situation for both the countries". Wages and incomes also increase due to specialization and increase efficiency in production and consumption, after the trade takes place. According to Ricardo, the benefit for both the countries will be more if they engage in free trade of goods & services in which those countries enjoy a comparative advantage.

"Heckscher-Ohlin model" proposes that "trade enhances welfare for the nations engaged as they experience higher levels of aggregated utility as compared to autarky". Apart from this, "the countries relatively abundant factors gain from the trade and the relatively scarce factors lose. When the gains surpass the loses, the welfare takes place" (Sunronovic, 2009)

"Krugman and Obstfeld (2006)" stated that "in the short run, factors of those industries which must compete with imports tend to lose from the trade". However, in the more extended period, "a country's scarce factors lose from trade and a redistribution of income takes place. In the end, gains outweigh the losses, and overall gains from trade should be expected." (Krugman and Obstfeld, 2006)

As mentioned by J.F. Mejia (2011), another theory by Leibenstein proposes that the efficiency levels are influenced by the competition, because the competition and adversity create some pressure to change. These pressures are likely to lead to efforts towards cost savings, which are absent in the ordinary course. In such cases, the higher the incentive to change, the higher will be the success rate of the firms in reducing their costs to the minimum levels. Thus, going by this theory, one may deduce that trade increases competition and thus increases countries managerial and productive effort.

Helpman & Krugman (1985) have tried to answer the question of "Intra industry trade", in other words, "two-way trade in similar goods" between two countries as arising out of monopolistic competition as well as economies of increase in scale and such "two-way trade happens in differentiated products".

Falvey and Kierzkowski (1987) have proposed a rationale for the international exchange of goods which appear similar but differ in quality because of different proportion of production factors used in production of those goods. For example, the goods which use capital intensive technology, manufacturing methods have a higher quality compared to the goods which are less capital intensive.

Balassa (1965) had propounded the theory of revealed comparative advantage, according to which "countries specialize and export those goods which they can produce at lower costs compared to the world" (Balassa, 1965). The RCA of a country in different goods depends on the "physical and human capital endowments of the country". As technology progresses, such endowments can undergo a change and the countries RCA also changes accordingly over some time as they engage in trade and specialize.

Further studies by Krugman and Obstfeld (2006) proposes that trade is beneficial as it increases market size "even between countries with similar technology and factor endowments". This theory states that a larger market opens up due to trade, and it results in "lower average prices and availability of a large variety of goods increasing welfare".

"Grubel, Lloyd (1975)" suggested, "Intra-industry trade" between two countries in terms of differentiated goods both similar as well as complementary goods that could occur at different stages of a manufacturing process which is otherwise called as production fragmentation.

2.2 TRADE BETWEEN INDIA AND ASEAN

Several studies have explored the nature and extent of the trade between "India and ASEAN countries". Radhika Kak (2014) presented that "India's exports to ASEAN have increased by 11x, while total Indian exports have risen only 6x during the past 10 years (2003-2013)". Indian exports to ASEAN are likely to reach $280 bn in the next 10 years (by 2023) which means a CAGR of 24% compared to 22% in the past 10 years. The study also finds that India has an "advantage in chemicals, pharmaceuticals, gems & jewellery, iron&steel and other services, whereas ASEAN has advantages in Natural resources and electronics".

Keya Chaturvedi (2014) states that China's industrial sector has achieved higher growth than the country's GDP when compared to India's slower rate of growth in the industrial sector. This could be because of India's hesitant approach to liberalizing the economy in key sectors such as banking and insurance. The study highlighted trade barriers faced by Indian companies in both Banking and Insurance. The study hoped that the proposed FTAs in China could be used to address some issues of India, "Look East Policy", "Bangladesh-China-India-Myanmar Trade Corridor (BCIM)", "Regional Comprehensive Economic Partnership (RCEP)", and the bilateral FTA are among initiatives in this direction.

"Department of Commerce has consciously worked on diversifying our export markets, reducing the dependence on traditional markets...India has been pursuing market diversification policies directing her export promotion efforts at Asia and ASEAN, Latin America and Africa through Focus Market initiatives and bilateral trade agreements" (Department of Commerce 2014)

Another Study by Radha Raghuramapatruni (2012) finds that the "Trade intensity between India and ASEAN has not only increased and India's exports to and imports from ASEAN countries are intense compared to the trade pattern with rest of the world". Also, "there are greater complementarities" between exports of India and ASEAN countries as reflected by RCA Index (revealed comparative advantage index). Hence. "there is great potential for an increase in trade intensity, which could be the result of the policies adopted by the Indian government since early 1990 and the Look East policy".

Shankaran Nambiar (2011)'s paper attempts to look beyond the trade in goods to find "other areas that could offer scope for broader engagement between India and ASEAN in future". As India became "globally competitive in the production of pharmaceuticals, stronger cooperation with ASEAN states might increase India's export value in health products and healthcare systems in many countries of ASEAN. An essential aspect in this is the provision of affordable generic and other drugs for diseases such as HIV (human immunodeficiency virus) and AIDS (acquired immune deficiency syndrome) in ASEAN states – as generic drugs are much cheaper than branded drugs and therefore a highly attractive import product". The study categorically mentions that "services, security, environment and infrastructure offer wider opportunities for future collaboration", based on the assumption that

ASEAN countries have a comparative advantage in manufacturing while India has in services.

Daniel Jacobius Morgan (2012) mentioned that India could import from ASEAN countries many products that are currently being imported from China. By doing so, India can reduce its bilateral trade deficit with China that can result in an equal trading relation. According to UN data, India currently imports more than 50% of its imports in 36 product categories from China. India needs to find more sources for these products for trade security and diversification. India is also heavily dependent on chemical imports from China, which are essential to make fertilizers. In 2011, "India imported more than 50% of chemicals such as nitrogen compounds, heterocyclic compounds, and metallic salts from China" (Daniel Jacobius Morgan 2012). ASEAN countries can offer to export such type of chemicals to India to begin diversifying import sources to ASEAN.

Dr Pradeep Kumar (2012), opined that initially "ASEAN countries regarded India as a useful partner to balance China's military power", but later ASEAN has come to realize that it is necessary to integrate cooperation with two regional emerging economic powers India and China. Eventually, "China began to view India as a new contributor to East Asian cooperation, strengthening the trend of multipolarity in Asia and Asia-Pacific. Nevertheless, there are differences in perceptions and interests between China and India in their ties with ASEAN. The geopolitical factor and rise of China and India have made them competitors for ASEAN's favour from visible trade and investment for their domestic modernization to invisible cooperation and support for their increasing international influence."

C Nalin Kumar maintains that "India's trade intensity with ASEAN may not be significant. However, commodity-wise importance should be given, and appropriate trade facilitation measures are taken, such as mutual recognition agreements. Since ASEAN has a better standing on this, this would serve in enhancing trade".

USITC publication on ASEAN (2010) states that some of the ASEAN countries have attracted foreign investments in the healthcare industry, mainly from countries such as India, Korea and China. This became possible because of the rapidly growing pharmaceutical &medical device markets, low production costs and tax exemptions/ investments offered by these governments to foreign investors.

Vinayak HV (2014) further states that "Together ASEAN's ten member states form economic powerhouse, ASEAN is not a monolithic market, Growth is provided by Macroeconomic stability, growing hub of consumer demand, and well-positioned for global trade inflows, Interregional trade could significantly deepen, but there are hurdles, it is home to several globally competitive companies" (Vinayak HV 2014)

The World Bank report (2013), commenting about the disadvantages of the MFNs (Most favored nations) etc which are results of the Preferential Trade agreements (PTA), opined that these may be useful among the developing countries for those "wishing to 'deepen' their integration in other spheres of economic cooperation beyond trade and thereby may strengthen their future participation in global co-operative efforts".

2.3 CONCERNS AND ISSUES IN TRADE BETWEEN INDIA AND ASEAN

NTBS and NTM: "Mohammed Saquib & Nisha Taneja (2005)" examined the impact of NTB (non-tariff barriers) on "India's exports to ASEAN and Srilanka" during the period 1998-99 to 2002-2003. The methodology adopted was to measure the incidence of NTM (non-tariff measure) using Frequency Index, finding the no of instances certain transactions were subject to NTM. A second index was also calculated to see the share of total imports subject to NTM. Other than the secondary data analysis thus obtained, the authors have also done a survey of 250 firms in different categories of product lines facing NTBs and concluded based on the observations that there was an increase in NTMs. An interesting point that emerged out of the survey was "that a larger proportion of smaller firms had faced more NTBs" compared to the more prominent firms. "Similarly, a smaller proportion of firms with a foreign affiliation have faced NTBs" compared to those without foreign affiliation.

Niru Yadav (2010) discussed the potential benefits of AIFTA, signed in August 2009 between "India and ASEAN" countries. This is an important milestone in India's "Look East Policy"; however, according to the author, the economic gains will be substantial if there is a focus on "Intra Industry Trade". The author felt that the goods covered by the agreement give enough scope to increase supply chain integration in machinery, electric and electronics sectors. This could be further supported if service trade and related investment are also included in the agreement, subject to other factors including reduction in NTBs, increase in business to business communication and harmonization of standards.

Smitha Francis (2011) argued that the FTA between ASEAN and India could impact the Indian agricultural sector negatively with cheaper import substitutes from ASEAN countries, especially in processed agricultural products. However, import liberalization under the FTA could impel MNCs "to undertake production rationalization across the region, and that could lead to deeper production integration in segments such as chemicals, machinery and transport equipment." The author opines that due to increased production networks and "consequent decline in the need for setting up more production units in India could adversely affect the welfare aspects" such as employment and livelihood.

Suthiphand Chirathivat et al. (2012) analyzed that, of late, "Asian International Production Network has emerged rapidly, and it was called as 'Factory Asia' where China acted as global assembly centre and ASEAN countries involved in the production networks in the supply chain". The paper also observes from the data of trade in intermediate goods that share of India in ASEAN, especially in this context is lower compared to that of China, although it is steadily increasing. Further, the paper argues that for deeper integration of production networks, connectivity issues such as transportation need to be sorted out, and multimodal, multi-functional and multi-tier approach is required.

Witada Anukoonwattka et al. (2011) in their compilation of studies in trade and investment, argued that India's focus is still focused on traditional finished goods exports to ASEAN and consequently India could not take full advantage of the Production networks developed in ASEAN region, unlike China. This requires further actions to support Indian export-oriented units which use labour cost advantage and increase competitiveness. The need for efficiency primarily drives FDI in the International production networks, hence building those efficiencies would attract FDI in this sector, thus enabling India to take advantage of the intraregional networks.

According to Mitsuyo Ando (2006), traditionally "East Asian trade was dominated by Inter-industry trade between North-South East Asian countries earlier produced and exported labour-intensive and resource-based products and Japan exported a wide range of manufactured products". The empirical data shows that after 1990, this has changed and "vertical Intra Industry trade" has increased in the region more so in machinery parts and components, compared to machinery products. Since the data suggested that the vertical IIT thus observed did not result from 'Quality ladder', "because the vertical IIT exports in higher-income countries did not have higher prices and that lower-income countries are not with lower prices as in the case of the traditional vertical IIT in quality differentiated products", hence these phenomena is due to the fragmentation in production chains and back and forth transactions. The methodology used to get this conclusion involved a calculation of threshold-based index for (i) one-way trade (ii) horizontal IIT and (iii) vertical IIT. "The threshold-based index of each East Asian economy is calculated for the trade of each machinery sector, i.e., general machinery, electric machinery, transport equipment, and precision machinery, as well as for machinery trade as a whole" Mitsuyo Ando (2006).

Prema-chandra Athukorala (2010), in his paper, concluded that Global production sharing had played an important role in East Asia. Rapid integration into regional production networks by China has led to the fragmentation and specialization in trade, especially in ASEAN countries. As the exports of China to extra-regional markets have multiplied, the imports of intermediate goods, parts & components from regional networks has also increased simultaneously. This was evident in the remarkable contraction of trade in the last quarter of 2008, following the world financial crisis.

According to Meenu Tiware et al. (2015), A deeper integration into East Asia / ASEAN is affected due to several factors including "large domestic market taking preference over exports, low-value addition in the manufacturing sector, other impediments related to lack of scale, quality inputs, R&D skills etc. India's share of exports in parts and consumables was negligible compared to that of ASEAN countries and China". The undertakes to find the reason for the inadequate integration of India into the regional production networks as well as the structural problems that make Indian manufacturing less efficient, by quantitative and qualitative tools and techniques. "Grubel-Lloyd index" was employed to calculate bilateral "Intra Industry Trade". The findings include that although "there was steady growth in India's integration with global production networks, India's intermediate products has gone much faster than the aggregate manufactured goods under the study period". India's exports have shown "a bias in favour of final goods than parts and components (P&C)." Also, there was a shift in India's exports towards capital intensive and natural resource-intensive products than labour-intensive traditional products. India's trade balance has become surplus in final manufactured goods and negative in P&C, indicating that the increased assembly activity in India is partly due to an increase in domestic consumption. Also, India imported intermediates with unit values higher than its exports in the same category. Finally, the conclusion was that "India has significant potential to expand its ASEAN export share in the machinery sector, while also building on its existing strength in the chemicals sector". It is also mentioned in a footnote that there is a two-way trade in organic chemicals as both exports and imports from India to ASEAN have seen significant growth in this period.

Niru Yadav (2010) observed that the benefits of AIFTA would be substantial if there is a focus on "Intra industry trade". He also pointed out that the AIFTA has given scope to increase in supply chain integration in machinery, electric and electronics sectors.

ASSOCHAM's report (July 2016) states that the total bilateral trade between India and ASEAN has increased more than threefold from US$21 bn in 2005-06 to US$65 bn in 2015-16. However, the report concludes with a categorical remark that "There is no denying that the ASEAN India Free Trade Agreement brings strategic gains to India; however, economic gains can be substantial only if supply chains are developed with a focus towards intra-industry trade." Further, the report summarizes that "Indo ASEAN economic engagement should not be viewed from a pure merchandise trade perspective, but from the future potential of trade in services and investment flows. Trade is not a negative-sum game it brings with it benefits of lower input prices, greater competition and a virtuous cycle of rising productivity and growth" (ASSOCHAM, 2016)

ALLEYNE, Antonio, LORDE, Troy (2014) studied the trade among 'CARICOM' member states using panel data gravity model, using 'Fixed Effects Model (FEM)'. They examined whether GDP, Per Capita GDP, Population and distance or remoteness of member countries have an impact on the trade performance among the member states in the Caribbean region. The results of their study conclude that these variables have significant importance in trade performance. Apart from the positive correlation between trade GDP, the negative correlation between distance or remoteness to the trade performance is significant, thus advocating that the member states should focus on enhancing the trade with geographically closer countries in order to improve the trade.

Sabyasachi Tripathi and Nuno Carlos Leitao (March 2013) examined India's trade with 20 countries using static and dynamic panel data, with gravity model. They found that factors such as "political globalization" and "cultural proximity" have a positive impact on the trade as well as the size of economies and the common border between countries. The 'political globalization' between trading partners is consisting of embassies in the countries and membership in an international trade association. Similarly, 'cultural proximity' is measured by variables such as the number of MacDonald's restaurants per capita. Their findings suggest that the economy size variables, such as GDP per capita, have a positive influence on India's bilateral trade with other countries. According to their analysis, the geographical proximity between India and trade partners could impact the bilateral trade more in case of the major trading partners.

3

ASEAN as a Regional Block

Before making a detailed study on India and ASEAN trade relations, it would be in the fitness of things to present a brief account on the regional block "Association of South –East Asian nations", and its growing significance to become a dynamic force in Asia and a review of the developments of India's relation with the regional grouping. Thus, in this context, the subject is dealt in four sections in this chapter. The objectives of the chapter are given in the first section; section two portrays the formation of the regional grouping ASEAN, Socio-Economic Indicators and brief profiles of the ASEAN-5 nations. Section three studies the progress in relations between India and ASEAN, "India's Look East Policy", and the potentiality of trade between the two regions and the conclusion is given in the last section.

3.1. OBJECTIVES

1. To study the background of the formation of regional grouping ASEAN.
2. To assess the overall trends in major socio-economic indicators of 10 nations of the ASEAN.
3. To evaluate prospects of growth in India's relation with the regional grouping.

3.2 ASEAN AS A REGIONAL BLOCK

The ten membered "Association of the South East Asian Nations (ASEAN)" (asean.org) came into existence on August 8, 1967, through "Bangkok Declaration" among major Southeast Asian countries, namely "Singapore, Malaysia, Indonesia, Thailand, and the Philippines" and from then onwards, the regional grouping has grown to be one among fastest developing regional blocs in the world. Subsequently, the other five countries of East Asia joined the Regional Block. Brunei joined ASEAN in 1984, followed by Vietnam during 1995 and Laos and Myanmar during 1997, and the last one to join was Cambodia in 1999. For the past five decades, ASEAN has made remarkable momentum both in economic and social terms, reduced gaps in development among ASEAN countries. The leaders of ASEAN have signed a declaration at "27the Summit meeting in Kuala Lumpur" in November 2015 to form "ASEAN". This declaration was aimed at building of ASEAN Community in the following 10 years. The roadmap articulates goals of ASEAN countries to consolidate and integrate their economies and to make a cohesive community. Today economy of "ASEAN" has seen steady growth for the past fifty years and increased by a hundred times since its formation, and by 2016, it has reached a combined Gross Domestic Product of 2.55 trillion US dollars, contributed 6.2% of the Gross Domestic Product of the world (on the basis of US dollars at Purchasing Power Parity). In 2016, ASEAN had become 6th biggest economy globally and 3rd biggest economy in Asia in terms of its total GDP. The reach of ASEAN in economic terms would be more substantial, combined with dialogue partners and sectoral partners. The primary reason for the existence of ASEAN as an economic region is to achieve growth and development, both social and cultural, security and peace in the region in the resolve of unity and partnership.

Figure: 3.2

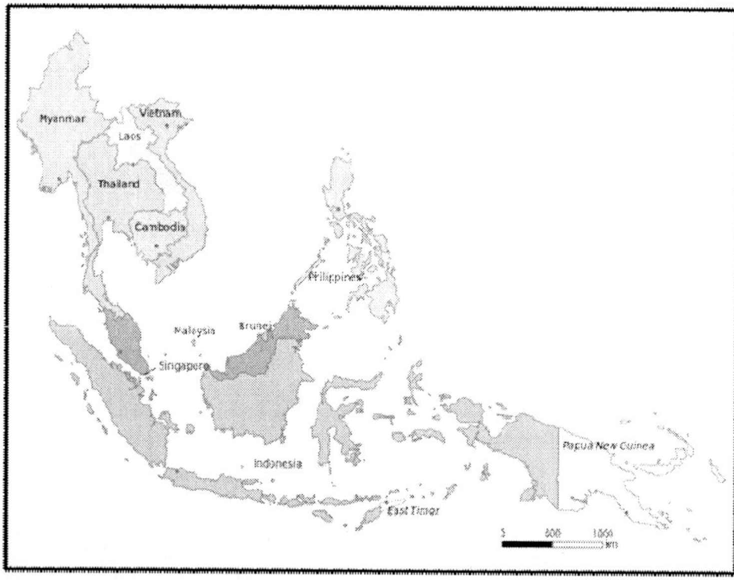

However, the association has made unbalanced improvement since the "Bangkok declaration (1967)" that created space for the formation of ASEAN, especially during the initial phase, due to the strategic and political differences. A beginning in the ASEAN economic cooperation was made since1976, after "Treaty of Amity and Cooperation in South East Asia" has been signed, and "The Preferential Trading Arrangement" is declared(asean.org). According to Atul Sharma et al., "The Preferential Trade Agreement (PTA), however, did not succeed because of low preference margins (20-23 per cent tariff reductions) and the exclusion of essential imports of member states from the preferential treatment list. Even with the increase of the preference margins to 50 per cent, reduction of the ASEAN content requirement from 50 to 35 per cent, more extensive coverage of products (15,000) and reduction in non-tariff trade barriers in 1987 under the enhanced PTA program, the intra-trade in the

ASEAN member countries did not grow much. There were attempts during the 1980s to promote cooperation among the member states, such as AIP (Asian Industrial Projects), AIJVS (Asian Industrial Joint Ventures) but they also have met with a similar fate".

This was followed by liberalization policies being adopted by a few member states including Indonesia, Thailand, Philippines and Malaysia during the late eighties, which allowed taking more significant steps towards concretizing the economic efforts for greater cooperation. "ASEAN Free Trade Area Cooperation and Intellectual Property Rights and Industrial Cooperation" (asean.org) were introduced during the 1990s.

"The Framework Agreement on Enhancing Economic Cooperation" (1992) (asean.org) has proposed "ASEAN Free Trade Area (AFTA)" to increase cooperation among ASEAN members states and enhance its combined strength in the world market. Apart from the goods, services such as tourism, financial, shipping, logistics, construction and telecommunication were included in AFTA in December 1995. This was followed by envisioning ASEAN Vision 2020 in 1997 to further the economic integration among member states. Vision 2020 aims at making ASEAN a stable, competitive and vibrant economy where free trade of goods, services and investments is followed, thus leading equitable distribution of wealth and social justice.

ASEAN has seen success in getting market access to major economies such as Japan, Europe and the USA by using collective bargaining power. ASEAN economies are among the most successful in development. "Though the ASEAN members have internal differences, they have an ideological affinity to the west and common anti-communist policy posture." Further, due to the high resource endowment, ASEAN has achieved higher growth. It turned into major centres of global trade and investment.

3.2.1. Objectives of ASEAN according to "The ASEAN Declaration."

- "To accelerate the economic growth, social progress and cultural development in the region through joint endeavours in the spirit of equality and partnership in order to strengthen the foundation for a prosperous and peaceful community of Southeast Asian nations," (asean.org) and
- "To promote regional peace and stability through abiding respect for justice and the rule of law in the relationship among countries in the region and adherence to the principles of the United Nations Charter."(asean.org)

"ASEAN Economic Cooperation" covers all the segments including investment, trade, manufacturing, agriculture, tourism and services. The following plans guide Their functional cooperation:

- "ASEAN Plan of Action on Social Development;
- ASEAN Plan of Action on Culture and Information;
- ASEAN Plan of Action on Science and Technology;
- ASEAN Strategic Plan of Action on the Environment;
- ASEAN Plan of Action on Drug Abuse Control; and
- ASEAN Plan of Action in Combating Transnational Crime"

(Source: asean.org)

3.2.2. Structures and Mechanism of the ASEAN

The top-most authoritative body of ASEAN is the "ASEAN Summit", and it is conducted annually. The meeting of the foreign ministers, namely "The ASEAN Ministerial Meeting" also is conducted every year. The working of ASEAN is done through Ministerial meetings on various trade sectors. Technical working groups and senior officials assist the ministerial committees. ASEAN also has established diplomatic missions to various countries such as USA, Britan, European countries, Japan, India, Russia, China and Pakistan.

Figure: 3.2.2.

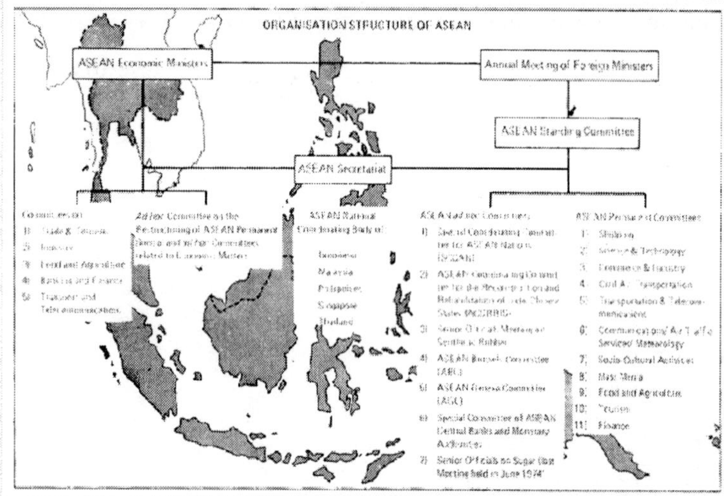

"The Secretary-General of ASEAN" coordinates the activities of ASEAN. There are specialized bodies and inter-governmental institutions such as "ASEAN University Network, ASEAN-EC Management Centre, ASEAN Centre for Energy, ASEAN Agricultural Development Planning Centre, ASEAN Specialized Meteorological Centre, ASEAN Tourism Information Centre, and ASEAN Timber Technology Centre. ASEAN-Chambers of Commerce and Industry, ASEAN Business Forum, ASEAN Tourism Association, ASEAN Council on petroleum, ASEAN Ports Association, ASEAN Vegetable Oils Club, and the ASEAN-Institutes for Strategic and International Studies." (asean.org)

3.3 ASEAN'S ECONOMY

ASEAN region has progressed tremendously over the past 50 years after it is formed, both in terms of economic and social aspects. This has also reduced disparities in development among the different nations in the region and promoted cooperation among them.

The ASEAN region expanded more than a hundred times economically since it was formed, and its combined Gross Domestic Product had gone up to 3 trillion US dollars in 2017. Since 1999, when ASEAN achieved its full 10 member participation, the growth has been four-fold until 2017, and the region's economy has become 6th biggest globally and 3rd biggest in Asia. Standard of living also has gone up during the year 2017 with its GDP four times more than the level in the year 1999, the year ASEAN had full membership with 10 countries. In 2017, ASEAN had become 6th biggest economy globally and 3rd biggest economy in Asia in terms of its total GDP. There was a notable improvement in living standards with per-capita income growing up to US$5236 in 2017 from just US$122 in 1967.

Table 3.1 Evolution of ASEAN's Economy over the Past 50 years- Select Indicators

Indicators	- 1967	1984	1995	1997	1999	2005	2010	2016	2017
GDP at current prices (US$ Trn)	0.02	0.22	0.65	0.72	0.58	0.94	1.93	2.55	2.89
GDP Growth Rate (%)	4.3	4.4	8.1	4.5	3.4	5.8	7.5	4.8	5.3
% Share of ASEAN in World GDP (% based on US$ at PPP)	3.3	3.6	5.1	5.3	4.8	5.2	5.6	6.2	7.4
GDP per capita (US$ at current prices)	122	765	1,556	1,462	1,135	1,701	3,268	4,021	5,236

Source: ASEAN Secretariat

There was considerable progress in the distribution of income in the ASEAN region over the past 20 years. ASEAN has achieved the "Millennium Development Goal (MDG)" by 2015, the US$1.25 per day line of poverty and continues to improve the earnings of the lowest of income groups.

"The income gap among different member states of ASEAN is reducing: the GDP per capita of the most prosperous country was 131 times larger than that of the poorest country in 2005; it was reduced to 60 times in 2010, and it will be only 47 times by 2018. Higher growth registered in small countries narrows this gap." (asean.org)

3.3.1 ASEAN's International Trade

"The growing significance of international trade as a growth facilitator for the region is visible from the performance of ASEAN countries over the years. ASEAN's total trade accounts for a 7.1 per cent share of the world's total trade, and it is the fourth-largest trading region in the world, behind the European Union, USA and China." (Exim Bank, 2018). Total merchandise trade of ASEAN marked up 3.5 times to 2574 billion US dollars in 2017 from 790 billion US dollars in 2000.

Table.3.2

Evolution of ASEAN's International Trade-Select Indicators

Indicators	1967	1984	1995	1997	1999	2005	2010	2016	2017
% Share of ASEAN in the World Exports	2	3.9	5.8	6.3	6.2	6.2	6.9	7.2	7.42
% Share of ASEAN in the World Imports	2.3	3.6	6.1	6.4	5	5.3	6.2	6.6	6.99
Trade to GDP ratio (%)	43.1	69.3	96.7	100	113	131	104	87	93.1

Source: Data extracted from ASEAN Secretariat

The share of exports of ASEAN in world exports has gradually risen from 2% from 1967 to 7.42% in 2017, i.e., more than three times in the last 50 years. Similarly, the share of imports also increased from 2.3% in 1967 to 6.9% in 2017. (Table. 3.2).

3.3.2 Intra-ASEAN Trade

"ATiGA (ASEAN Trade in Goods Agreement)," (asean.org), manages the trade that happens among the member nations of ASEAN since it was formed in 2010. The trade among the member states is the most significant component of ASEAN trade.

Table 3.3 Trends in Intra-ASEAN Trade

Indicators	1995	1997	1999	2005	2010	2016	2017
% Share of Intra-ASEAN in ASEAN's exports	23.1	24.1	21.1	25.3	28.1	24.7	23.5
% Share of ASEAN in the World Imports	16.5	17.6	19.6	24.5	26.4	22.2	22

Source: Based on the data extracted from ASEAN Secretariat

Trade among the member states of ASEAN, both in exports and imports has seen a gradual rise during the first 10 years from 1995, with an accelerated growth during the period 2001 to 2010, slowed down after 2010 due to global financial crisis.

"Intra-ASEAN" exports, when calculated as a percentage of ASEAN's overall exports, has shown an increasing trend from 1995 onwards with its maximum at 28% in 2010. The same trends with higher increase are observed in imports of "Intra-ASEAN" as a proportion of imports of the world from ASEAN region from 2001 to 2013, slow growth during 2014-17 in line with the global trends.

3.3.3 ASEAN Service Sector: Emerging outlook

As evidenced in other developing nations, ASEAN economies also are changing to more service-oriented economies. In this process, the advancement of institutions and competitiveness were crucial for ASEAN economies. Services trade has become all-pervasive and essential in the global economy and more so in production and supply chain networks. Services consisted of about half of the region's GDP in the last century and hit 53.1% in 2016 (Chart 3.1).

For the past decade (2006-2017), the service sector's performance in ASEAN member country economies, in terms of GDP, has grown in each country anywhere between 2 and 4 %. Malaysia has seen the highest growth, with 7.6%. Myanmar and Indonesia came next with 4.7 and 4.5% respectively.

Chart. 3.1

ASEAN International Trade in Services (US$ billion)

Source: Author's Calculation based on the data extracted from ASEAN Secretariat

3.3.4 Foreign Direct Investment Scenario in the ASEAN

ASEAN has seen remarkable growth with inflows of FDIs during troubled times in global financial markets. The inflow of FDI into ASEAN region has been rising since 2010, despite some fluctuations and downs in a few years, to 137 billion US dollars in 2010 from 108.2 billion US dollars in 2010. There were some differences in the way different sectors and sub-sectors have attracted the investments, but on the whole, the region had a good influx of foreign capital.

Chart. 3.2

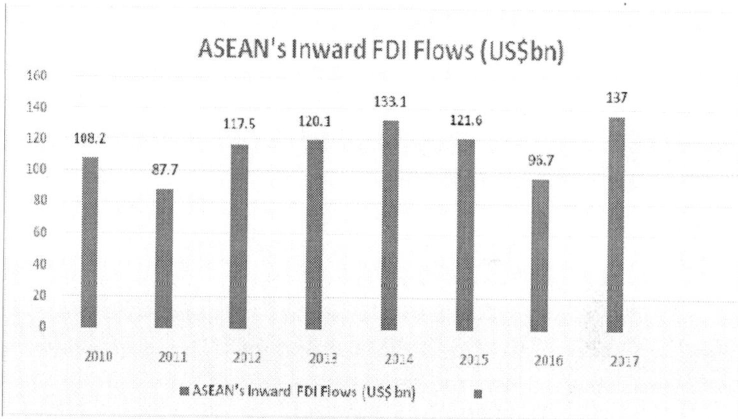

"Source: Author's Calculation based on the data extracted from ASEAN Secretariat."

The FDI inflow into ASEAN region as a whole, recorded a CAGR of 11.4% from 1984 to 2017, from a mere US$ 3 billion to US$137 billion. This was a significant performance despite adverse global financial market conditions and the drop in investment levels worldwide. The last 10 years, 2007 to 2017, have seen an increase in foreign investments more than two times.

Chart.3.3

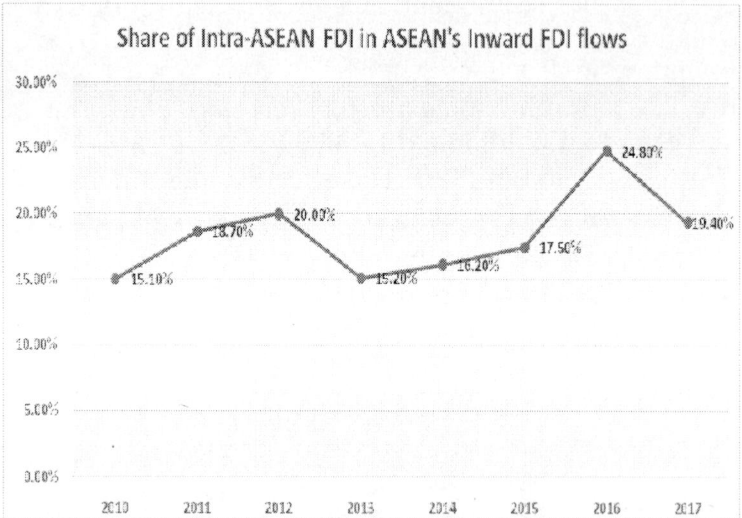

"Source: Authors' calculation based on the data extracted from ASEAN Secretariat."

Inflows of foreign capital into ASEAN member states from investors within the ASEAN countries are called "Intra-ASEAN" FDI. Initially, the share of such internal FDI flows was meagre but started growing from 2010 onwards and constituted 15.1 % of total FDI in 2010, grown to 24.8% in 2016 and subsequently were at 19.6% in 2017.

3.4 "ASEAN COMMUNITY VISION 2025".

The ASEAN member countries have formulated "ASEAN Community Vision 2025" which is also known to be ***"Kuala Lumpur Declaration on ASEAN 2025: Forging Ahead Together"***(asean.org), and it was accepted by all their leaders at "27th Summit in Kuala Lumpur, Malaysia". The vision document lays the path for the following 10 years to construct "ASEAN Community" which is "politically cohesive, economically integrated, and socially responsible" (asean.org). The vision conveyed in "ASEAN 2025" document is the result of in-depth deliberations, and it represents an outline of the Member States' decision for going ahead with ASEAN's evolvement into the next level.

3.4.1 "Master Plan on ASEAN Connectivity 2025"

Member states of ASEAN are getting attention through high growth and developing economies. Local enterprises in ASEAN member states becoming more competitive by enhancing their capacities and growing up the value chain. For the reduction of trade barriers, it is required to improve the connectivity in the region and facilitate ASEAN partners to establish solid enterprises in the region.

Given this background, the ASEAN leaders have endorsed "Master Plan on ASEAN Connectivity 2025 (MPAC 2025)" in September 2016. "The MPAC 2025, which succeeds in the Master Plan on ASEAN Connectivity 2010, focuses on five strategic areas: sustainable infrastructure, digital innovation, seamless logistics, regulatory excellence, and people mobility. The MPAC 2025 was developed in consultation with relevant ASEAN Sectoral Bodies and other stakeholders. The remaining initiatives from MPAC 2010 were evaluated and incorporated in the MPAC 2025." (Asean.org, 2016)

3.5 OVERVIEW OF ASEAN MEMBER STATES

Before a discussion of India's efforts to integrate with ASEAN, it is reasonable to have a look at the social, cultural, and economic status of each member state of ASEAN. A peek into such details about ASEAN member countries will give a broad understanding of the context in which these countries with seemingly different capabilities and endowments could come together and enact a decisive role in the economic progress of the region. Socio-economic indicators of each of the countries of ASEAN regional block are given in a table at the end of the section.

3.5.1 Singapore

A tiny multiracial island state, dangling with some fifty islets, Singapore is one of the world's great economic successes. Singapore is also known as 'The Lion City.' Historically, the two crucial factors that have formed the base of the Singapore economy are entrepot trade and the British Military. The specific geographical location of Singapore has enabled it to dominate the entrepot market in South East Asia. Especially the advantage of its location strategically placed at the south entrance of Malacca straits connecting the Indian ocean and Pacific-ocean. British dominance in the country and its policies have helped to gain political stability and free trade

The economic growth of Singapore has enabled it to develop socially and culturally. The socio-economic indicators of Singapore are presented in Table-3.4. Singapore's population is a racial mix with around 76 per cent Chinese, 15 per cent Malaysians and 6.5percent Indians, the rest being Eurasians and Europeans. The average growth rate of population in the1990s has been around 2.8 per cent per annum. The Government has been carefully monitoring the population to preserve the racial mix and the dependency ratio. General prosperity and excellent medical facilities available in the country have lowered infant mortality to 1 per thousand births and increased life expectancy to a male-female average of 83.2 years in 2017. With much importance given to education, literacy level increased to 95percent. The Singapore government provides most of the medical and health services, education, and housing to the people.

The country with a high standard of living and Human Development. (HDI is 0.932) Ranks 9th in the world (2018). It has a meagre (2 Percent) unemployment rate on average. Thus, Singapore is considered as one of the most prosperous nations among the ASEAN group.

Singapore has a natural advantage of its geographical locale, strategically placed in the sea routes between the Pacific Ocean and the Indian Ocean and near the straits of Malacca with a natural harbour. Colonial rule by the British had enabled political stability and due to which free trade and private industry have developed in the island nation, which became very successful in the trade.

Chart. 3.4 Singapore

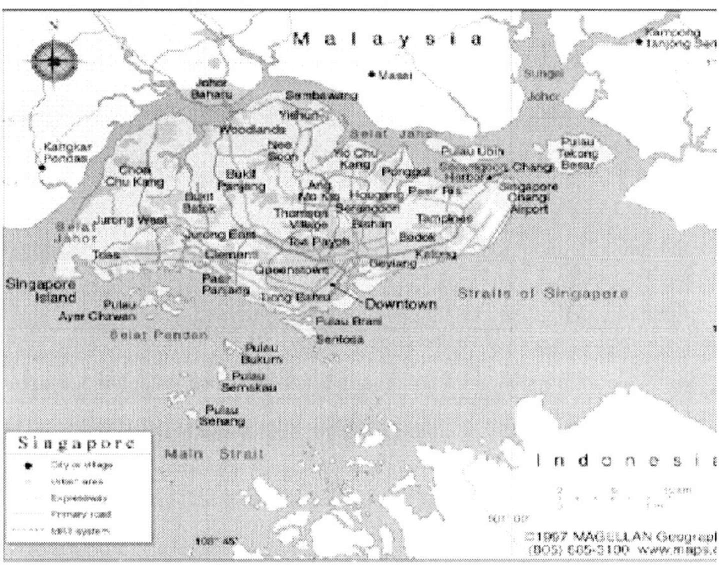

Singapore's population is a mix of 76% Chinese, 15% Malaysians, 6.5% Indians and rest from Eurasians and Europeans. High literacy rate at 97%, Low infant mortality at 3%, Life expectancy of 83 years- one of the highest, High standard of living with per capita GDP of US$52,962 and overall GDP of close to US$ 300 billion etc were result of sustained efforts by the government which made the country one of the most prosperous in the world.

Table. 3.4 Singapore: Socio-Economic Indicators

Economic Indicators	2012	2013	2014	2015	2016	2017	2018
GDP (US$ bn)	289.2	302.5	308.2	296.8	297	305.5	311
Real GDP growth (%)	3.9	5	3.6	1.9	2	2.9	2
Consumer price inflation (avg,%)	4.6	2.4	1	-0.5	-0.5	1.3	1.6
Population (mn)	5.3	5.4	5.5	5.5	5.6	5.7	5.8
Merchandise exports fob (US$ bn)	442.8	447.7	442.7	379.6	361.6	408.2	429.9
Merchandise imports fob (US$ bn)	371.6	372.6	360.9	296.7	278.8	317.8	341.3
Total int'l reserves (US$ bn)	259.3	273.1	256.9	247.8	246.6	266.3	271.6
Avg exchange rate (S$: US$)	1.25	1.25	1.27	1.14	1.38	1.4	1.42
Life Expectancy at Birth	80	80	81.9	82	83	83.2	83.2
GNI Per capita	45,228	51,367	57,709	71,689	78,742	78,427	82,503
Mean Schooling in Years	5.8	7.3	8.9	10.5	11.2	11.5	11.5
HDI Score	0.773	0.819	0.868	0.909	0.929	0.93	0.932

Source: World Development Report, WB; International Financial Statistics, IMF; Human Development Report, UNDP: Asian Development Outlook, ADB; Various Issues

The country is heavily dependent on foreign trade with services being the dominant sector with a contribution of 73.4% of the GDP in 2016. The country depends on imports for "foodstuffs, raw materials for the industry, fuel and capital goods". However, Singapore has a trade surplus and no external debts. There has been a steady increase in FDIs in Singapore from the US, Japan, and Europe. Singapore is also a prominent investor in ASEAN countries.

3.5.2 Indonesia

The Republic of Indonesia is spread over more than 13,677 islands and is rich in natural resources. Its large population and petroleum wealth give it the foundation to be a regional power. It remained a relatively poor country and achieved the status of a 'middle-income' country by World Bank Criteria, only in 1981, when its national income per capita first exceeded the threshold of US$ 500. There are, however, considerable inequalities in the distribution of per capita income. In Indonesia, the basis of development is petroleum. There are vast reserves of natural gas and oil, and Indonesia produces commodities such as pepper, rubber, cloves, tobacco, cloves, rubber, nutmeg, palm oil, tin, timber, tea and tobacco. Agriculture was the predominant sector in its economy in terms of produce until 1991, and later it was superseded by manufacturing. The industrialization has been given high priority since the takeover of the 'New Order' lead by President Suharto. The initial strategy was to establishing import-substituting enterprises. However, inefficiencies and high costs in production gave way to liberalizing reforms intended to improve the export potential of manufactured products. These measures proved very successful, and steady growth in manufactured exports has taken place since 1987.

Chart. 3.5 Indonesia

Indonesia's agriculture sector was predominant up to 1991, and later manufacturing sector gained an increase in its share due to industrialization. World Bank has categorised Indonesia a middle-income nation. The GDP is at US$932 billion, but the per capita GDP is US$3570 only. The country has made progress in the last 10 years to increase the literacy rate to approximately 95% however the life expectancy remained at 69 years.

Close to 80% of the country's export earnings are from Oil and natural gas, and this has given surplus initially to fund the country's ambitious plans to industrialize the economy. Although the export earnings have fluctuated along with fluctuations in the global oil market, its merchandise trade has always had a surplus. Other than petroleum products, the country also exports agricultural and mineral products such as rubber, coffee, shrimps, palm oil apart from few manufactured goods such as textiles and garments. The real GDP growth in Indonesia was 8% per annum in the 1970s and has been an average of 6.1 per cent between 1980-1990 and 4.2 per cent between 1990-2003 The cracking of oil prices in 1981 hit the economy severely as 80% of its total export revenues are from oil and natural gas. In 1996, the per capita GDP had reached a high of $1155, but due to a severe crash in GDP by 13.1 per cent in 1998, the per capita GDP also fell drastically touching a low of $483 per annum, even lower than the level in 1980. The composition of GDP has slightly changed over the years. Though the agricultural sector is the predominant in Indonesia, its contribution and has declined from 26 per cent of GDP in 1980 to 9.5 in 2003, and it was surpassed by manufacturing in 1991. The agricultural sector is divided into cash crops, food crops, fishing, forestry and animal husbandry- of which the food crops subdivision is the most important for the generation of employment and income.

In the industrial sector, the petroleum and natural gas industries have played an important role in providing Indonesia with resources to fund its developmental programs. Owing to the heavy dependence of the economy on such industries for both its foreign exchange and fiscal revenues, the country's prosperity is closely linked to fluctuations in international petroleum markets. In addition to natural gas and petroleum, Indonesia has reasonable reserves of minerals such as 'coal, tin, bauxite, copper, nickel, gold and silver". The Industrial sector's overall value addition to GDP has almost remained the same and was around 48.6 per cent in 2002.

Indonesia's share in world trade has remained around 1 %. Indonesia's exports were mainly occupied by revenues from crude petroleum and natural gas during the period 1970s to 1980s. Since 1986, however, the Indonesian Government has adopted a wide range of measures aimed at promoting the expansion of non-hydrocarbon exports, which changed the composition of its exports. Although

Table. 3.5 Indonesia: Socio-Economic Indicators

Indicators	2012	2013	2014	2015	2016	2017	2018
GDP (US$ bn)	917.7	912.3	890.5	861.1	932.1	1,021.50	1,070.00
Real GDP growth (%)	6	5.6	5	4.9	5	5.2	4.7
Consumer price inflation (avg, %)	4.3	6.4	6.4	6.4	3.5	4.4	5.7
Population (mn)	248.2	250.8	253.3	255.8	258.2	260.6	262.9
Merchandise exports f.o.b. (US$ bn)	187.3	182.1	175.3	149.1	144.4	155.6	154.9
Merchandise imports f.o.b. (US$ bn)	178.7	176.3	168.3	135.1	129	139.1	140.3
Total int'l reserves (US$ bn)	112.8	99.4	111.9	105.9	116.4	123.2	118.2
Avg exchange rate (Rp : US$)	9,387	10,461	11,865	13,389	13,308	13,370	13,969
Life Expectancy at Birth	77.4	78.3	80.2	81.9	82.8	83	83.2
GNI Per capita	45,228	51,367	57,709	71,681	78,742	78,427	82,503
Mean Schooling in Years	11.6	12.7	13.9	15.2	16.1	16.1	16.2
HDI Score	0.718	0.819	0.868	0.909	0.929	0.93	0.932

Source: World Development Report, WB; International Financial Statistics, IMF; Human Development Report, UNDP: Asian Development Outlook, ADB; Various Issues

export earnings declined during the early 1980s, the trade balance recorded a consistent surplus, as government policy measures, combined with a general slowing of economic activity led to reduced import demand. While Indonesia's merchandise trade balance has mostly shown a surplus, its trade in Invisibles has consistently shown a deficit at times more than offsetting the trade surplus. Apart from petroleum and gas, the country's other export products consist of primary and semi-processed agricultural and mineral commodities like rubber, coffee, shrimps, palm oil. In manufactured goods, textiles and garments also form an essential part of exports although their importance has been declining over the years. Indonesia's imports, meanwhile, have mainly consisted of capital goods and intermediate goods in recent years. Indonesia's trade was traditionally biased towards Japan, the USA, and Singapore. Its other leading trading partners are Germany and South Korea.

3.5.3 Malaysia

The federation of Malaysia, blessed with an abundance of natural resources, has immense economic potential. Modern Malaysia is in two parts, and the South China Sea separates the West and East. Together, they are the centre of a Malay sphere whose ethnic influence spreads along the 'Malay Peninsula' and then through the Malay Archipelago from Indonesia in the South to the Philippines in the North. In multi-racial Malaysia, where ethnic groups define politics, no government can take political harmony for granted.

Chart. 3.6 Malaysia

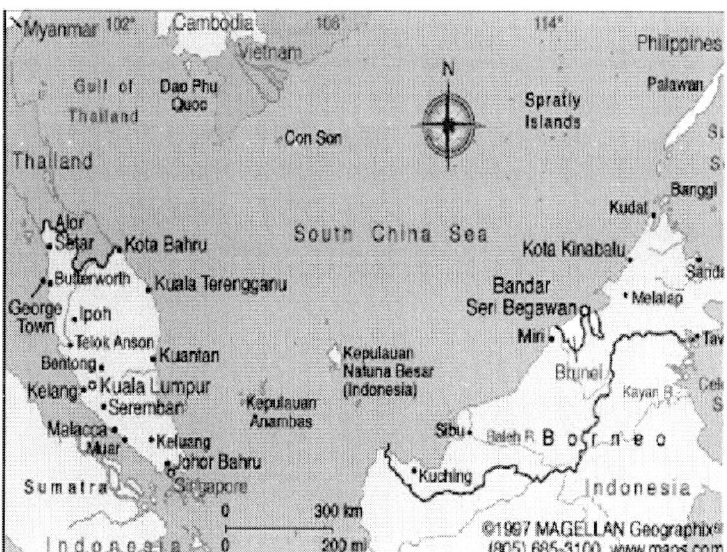

The social and economic indicators of Malaysia are given in Table-3.6 the country's population has been rising annually at 2.1 per cent on an average since 2003. The native Malays comprise 60 of the population. Economic clout, however, is wielded by the Chinese, who are about 30 per cent of the population; the Indians make up nearly 10 per cent of the people. Life expectancy had risen from 64 years in 1980 to nearly75.5 year in 2018, and infant mortality has fallen from 42 per thousand live births to 3.8. The mean schooling years increased to 10.2 in 2018. The HDI showed that Malaysia stood at 57th position out of 189 countries in overall human development in 2018 with a value of 0.802.

In the 1980s, the increase in external demand, boosted by the depreciation of the currency, thereby improving Malaysia's international competitiveness, was the main reason for the growth. The 1990s experienced exceptionally high growth rates, mainly due to the buoyant performance of the manufacturing, construction, and services sectors. Both the domestic market-oriented sector and the export-oriented sector experienced rapid growth during this period. As a consequence of the rapid growth in several segments of the economy, the service sector expanded, registering growth more than the overall GDP. For the first time, there was a 7.4 per cent decrease in GDP in 1998, a correction after continuous growth for 12 years, at an average of 7.8 per cent annually. The growth of all the sectors was adversely affected. The contraction was severely impacted manufacturing and construction segments. There was a recovery by 2003. Overall it was the significant government spending, directed towards agriculture, housing, education, infrastructure, which was the primary motive force to boost this growth.

Malaysia's GDP is US$320 billion, with per capita GDP at US$9508. The service sector dominates the economy with about 54% contribution. Among the

Table. 3.6 Malaysia: Socio-Economic Indicators

Indicators	2012	2013	2014	2015	2016	2017	2018
GDP (US$ bn)	314.4	323.3	338.1	296.4	296.5	302.7	320.3
Real GDP growth (%)	5.5	4.7	6	5	4.2	5.2	4.8
Consumer price inflation (avg, %)	1.7	2.1	3.1	2.1	2.1	3.9	2.5
Population (mn)	29.2	29.7	30.2	30.7	31.2	31.6	32
Merchandise exports fob (US$ bn)	208.8	202.3	207.5	174.6	165.3	188.2	201.2
Merchandise imports fob (US$ bn)	172.2	171.7	172.9	146.7	140.9	163.4	175.1
Total int'l reserves (US$ bn)	139.7	134.9	115.9	95.3	94.5	97.4	96.9
Avg exchange rate (M$: US$)	3.09	3.15	3.27	3.91	4.15	4.34	4.38
Life Expectancy at Birth	71.8	72.8	73.5	74.2	75.1	75.3	75.5
GNI Per capita	13,992	15,076	17,778	20,443	24,324	24,968	26,107
Mean Schooling in Years	7.6	8.6	7.6	9.8	10.2	10.2	10.2
HDI Score	0.683	0.725	0.731	0.772	0.795	0.799	0.802

Source: World Development Report, WB; International Financial Statistics, IMF; Human Development Report, UNDP; Asian Development Outlook, ADB; Various Issues.

industrial sector that contributes to about 30%, the electrical and electronic components industry contributes to the majority of export earnings. Apart from these, Malaysia is one of the prominent exporters of natural and agricultural resources such as rubber, palm oil as well as petroleum. According to the world economic forum report, Malaysia ranks 20th in the global competitiveness index and 19th in infrastructure such as quality roads, ports.

3.5.4 Philippines

One of Asia's wealthiest countries in the 1950s, Philippines, had become one of the poorest by the 1980s. The country's resources and potential remain enormous.

Recovery, for the Philippines, is, in essence, a political and social challenge to move from fundamentalism to stable democracy and to establish an economic system less distorted by corruption and feudalism. Statistical data of some of the underlying socio-economic indicators is given in Table-3.7. The population of the Philippines has increased steadily rate during the 1980s and 1990s, ranging between 2.2 - 2.7 per cent, which is among the highest increases in Asia. The expectancy of life has gone up from a male-female average of 62 years in 1980 to 69.2 years in 2018. Infant mortality had fallen from 81 per thousand live births in 1980 to 30 in 2018. A striking feature of the Philippines is the high literacy levels in comparison to other developing courtiers of Asia. The mean schooling years have increased from 6.6 during the year 2012 to 9.3 years during the year 2018. This is due to the great emphasis being given on education. The overall Human Development Index has gone up from 0.68 in 1980, to 0.699 in 2018, and the Philippines ranks 113 among 189 countries in terms of human development. The negative side is that due to massive increase in population, coupled with the constraint of land, that has caused significant migration to the urban areas, which have failed to provide enough new jobs, thus creating huge unemployment, underemployment is also very extensive, and is estimated to affect about one-quarter of the working population.

As seen in Table 3.6, the rate of growth in real GDP has declined from 6.6 in 2012 to 5.6 in the year 2018. During the 1980s, and the Philippines suffered significant and fundamental structural difficulties. Too much of protectionism, unequal distribution of wealth, resulting in narrow domestic market and inefficiencies due to 'crony capitalism,' badly affected productivity and rates of growth. The reform process from 1992 resulted in privatization, dismantling of domestic monopolies.

Chart 3.7 Philippines

Philippines share in world trade is presently around 0.8 per cent, and the composition of the Philippines export trade has been transformed since the 1970s. From being dominated by primary commodities, its composition has shifted in favour of manufacturing products such as electrical and electronic equipment, components, and garments. Changes in imports have been less, with capital equipment and intermediates occupying lions share. The invisible transactions of the Philippines have increased, and these invisible transactions partially offset the deficit on the merchandise account. The two principal sources of inflow are remittances from Filipinos working abroad, and tourists visiting the Philippines. Although total merchandise exports declined slightly in 1998, it showed positive growth from 1999. Imports, which also showed an increasing trend in the early 1990s, have shown a sharp decline in 1998 and continued to decline in 2002/ 2003. The fall in total trade in 1998 was the direct result of the economic crisis in East Asia, as Hongkong, Singapore, Japan, South Korea, which were also hit by the crisis, are its major partners in trade. Although total merchandise trade declined in 1998, it showed a positive performance in 1999 with significant earnings coming from manufactured exports led by the electronics sub-sector, machinery, and transport equipment. A substantial rollback happened when receipts from travel, investment and personal income have dropped. Another significant correction happened due to unpredictable currency

Table. 3.7 Philippines: Socio-Economic Indicators

Indicators	2012	2013	2014	2015	2016	2017	2018
GDP (US$ bn)	249.8	271.5	284.1	292.3	304.5	316.6	334.1
Real GDP growth (%)	6.6	7.1	6.1	6.1	6.9	6.5	5.6
Consumer price inflation (avg, %)	3.2	2.9	4.2	1.4	1.8	3	2.2
Population (mn)	96.9	98.5	100.1	101.7	103.3	104.9	106.5
Merchandise exports fob (US$ bn)	46.4	44.5	49.8	43.2	43.4	52.6	56.6
Merchandise imports fob (US$ bn)	65.3	62.2	67.2	66.5	77.5	90.3	94.9
Total int'l reserves (US$ bn)	83.8	83.2	79.5	80.7	80.7	83.3	83.4
Avg exchange rate (P: US$)	42.23	42.45	44.4	45.5	47.49	49.84	51.63
Life Expectancy at Birth	66.3	67.2	67.8	68.3	69	69.1	69.2
GNI Per capita(2011 PPP$)	4099	4972	5678	6754	8323	8729	9154
Mean Schooling in Years	6.6	7.1	8.7	8.9	9.3	9.3	9.3
HDI Score	0.598	0.621	0.65	0.665	0.693	0.696	0.699

Source: World Development Report, WB; International Financial Statistics, IMF; Human Development Report, UNDP: Asian Development Outlook, ADB; Various Issues.

situation, which led to a contraction of Peso value of deposits in foreign currency.

FDI in the Philippines has been relatively small compared to other Asia-Pacific countries. The rapid de-growth of the economy during 1983-85, however, precipitated by a political event, i.e., the assassination of President Aquino, which resulted in fall of the economy. It was only from 1993 that FDI inflow improved in the country in response to better economic and trade prospects, the primary recipient sectors being the food and cement industries. Some exceptions have been causing increased outflows, especially in short-term capital necessitated by secondary market-related non-repayments of trading bonds and commercial banks. There were also the borrowings by large public sector enterprises which resulted in debt servicing outflows.

However, the Philippines economy has great potential if it continues with its agrarian reforms, privatization, and improving the savings rate in order to fund domestic investment. This also means checking corruption; introducing accountability and changing the Philippine's work culture. Today the economy of the Philippines has 34th position in the world by with GDP of 348 billion US dollars. Philippines exports semiconductors, electronic equipment, transport machines, cloths, copper goods, petroleum goods, coconut oil, and fruits. Also, the country gets significant revenues from remittances from Filipinos settled abroad, tourism, and the BPO industry. Although the reports by Goldman Sachs and HSBC predicted the Philippines to be one among Asia's powerful economies, it is relatively underdeveloped with uneven growth and less developed transportation systems. The country is population is about 103 million and per-capita income is US$2951.

3.5.6 Thailand

Thailand is the only Asian country, which was not ruled by any western country directly, although France and the United Kingdom dominated it. Thailand is considered a newly industrialized country with the manufacture, agriculture, tourism being its leading sectors. The kingdom of Thailand, like its ASEAN partners, has abundant natural resources and has experienced a period of remarkable growth and structural change since 1996. Between 1986 and 1991, Thailand was one of the fast-growing countries. During this period the value of exports grew by 30 per cent per year and GDP at 9.2 per cent. The manufacturing sector has expanded significantly over the years. Thailand has seen somewhat of accelerated integration into the Asian and world economies since

Chart 3.8 Thailand

1985 and is being seen as a new model of development - one that is more relatable to the other less developed Asian economies. Some of its socio-economic trends can be seen from Table-3.8 Population was increasing at 1.4 per cent on an average between 1980 and 1990 and at 1 per cent average in the later years. Due to a well-implemented family welfare program, population growth is well under control. Thai society is a homogenous one with a one-third population consisting of ethnically Chinese people. Buddhism is more prevalent in the population with more than 80%, and a small Muslim

Table. 3.8 Thailand: Socio-Economic Indicators

Indicators	2012	2013	2014	2015	2016	2017	2018
GDP (US$ bn)	397.3	420.2	406.4	399.3	407.2	436.8	445.4
Real GDP growth (%)	7.2	2.7	0.9	3	3.3	3.3	2.6
Consumer price inflation (avg, %)	3	2.2	1.9	-0.9	0.2	0.8	0.9
Population (mn)	67.8	68.1	68.4	68.7	68.9	69	69.2
Merchandise exports fob (US$ bn)	227.7	227.5	226.6	214	214.3	228	233.4
Merchandise imports fob (US$ bn)	227.6	227.4	209.4	187.2	177.7	188.6	194.2
Total int'l reserves (US$ bn)	181.6	167.3	157.1	156.5	171.9	191.9	197.9
Avg exchange rate (Bt : US$)	31.1	30.7	32.5	34.2	35.3	34.3	35.3
Life Expectancy at Birth	70.2	70.6	72.1	73.9	75.1	75.3	75.5
GNI Per capita(2011 PPP$)	6,560	9,003	11,006	12,918	14,455	14,971	15,516
Mean Schooling in Years	4.6	5	6.1	7.6	7.7	7.6	7.6
HDI Score	0.611	0.649	0.693	0.724	0.741	0.748	0.755

Source: World Development Report, WB; International Financial Statistics, IMF; Human Development Report, UNDP: Asian Development Outlook, ADB; Various Issues

population (around 4 per cent) along the southern border is ethnically Malay.

Life expectancy rose from a male-female average of 63 years in 1980 to almost 75.5 years in 2018. Infant mortality had fallen from 58 per thousand births in 1980 to 5.6 in 2018. The mean years of schooling increased from 4.6 years from 2012 to 7.6 years during the year 2018. The overall "human development index" (HDI) shows a value of 0.755 in 2018, an increase from 0.645 in 1990. It stands 83rd among 189 nations in HDI ranking. The unemployment rate was 2.2 in 1990. It however sharply rose to 5.3 per cent in 1998 due to the of East Asia crisis, and after that declined to 1 per cent in 2018.

The structure of GDP has undergone a change where the relative share of agriculture has decreased, and that of industrial and services sector has increased. While agricultural value-added was 25 per cent of GDP in 1980, its contribution had declined to 8.4 per cent in 2018. In contrast, Industrial value-added went up to 39.2% in 2018 from 29%, and the service sector contribution is 52.4 % by the year 2018, mainly due to an increase in tourism and tourism-related services. Gross Domestic Savings went up to 36% of GDP in 1996 from 25% in 1980, and after that slightly fell. The rise was due to rising per capita incomes, and the fall in post-1996 was mainly due to the crisis resulting in a sharp decline in the exchange value of baht and high liquidity crunch. Gross Domestic Investment increased from 30 per cent of GDP in 1980 to nearly 42 per cent in 1996 due to the various monetary incentives given to encourage investment by domestic and foreign sources. The fall in GDI since 1997 is due to the overall pessimistic expectations, following the East Asian crisis, which was not conducive to investment activities.

Today overall the country recovered with a GDP of US$ 407 billion and per capita of GDP US$ 6729 during 2018 and FDI of 148.9$, the overall the challenge for Thailand is to put in place adequate infrastructure and upgrade its industries to avoid being undercut by cheaper labour from competitors such as India, Sri Lanka, Vietnam, and China. Exports contribute to two-thirds of its GDP with significant products such as computers, cars, electrical appliances, jewellery, textiles, footwear, fishery products, rice, and rubber, etc. Thailand has utilised the advantage of production networks of major MNCs, especially in vehicle manufacturing and assembly, components manufacturing. Thailand's automotive industry is said to be the largest in ASEAN and stood 9th largest globally. Moreover, its environment problems should be tackled if it wants to continue the growth in the tourism industry.

3.5.7 Laos PDR

Laos declared independent in 1953 from French colonization of about 60 years, but civil war ensued immediately after independence, and finally, the communist military government took power in 1975, ending the monarchy. The population consists of majority Laos about 55% followed by other local tribes and Mon-Khmer groups which account for the remaining population. However, despite economic reforms, the country has remained weak and dependent on aid from foreign countries.

Until the disintegration of Soviet bloc, Laos's foreign relations were hostile to the west, but later the country has opened to forge good relations with Australia, France, Japan, Turkey, Sweden, and the US apart from immediate neighbouring countries.

Chart 3.9 Laos PDR

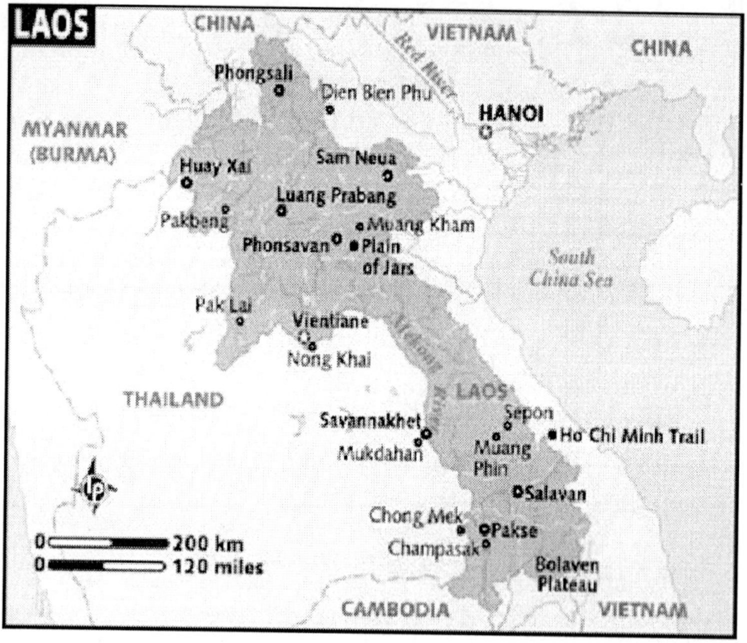

Most Laotians reside in rural areas, and about 80% depending on agriculture. The abundant water resources help the country to produce hydroelectricity and export to neighbouring countries. The state has huge ambitions in the hydropower sector, and it desires to become the "battery" of Southeast Asia. Laos GDP is at US$17.15 billion with per capita GDP at US$7400 (2017 estimates). Total FDI inflows are at 351.7 US$ million during the year 2018. Foreign Direct Investment from China, Thailand, and Vietnam have been flowing into the country, mainly in mining and hydropower sectors.

The literacy rate is 73% (2013 estimate), and the mean school enrolment ratio has increased from 3.6 years in 2012 to 5.2 years during the year 2018 and life expectancy stood at approximately 67 years during the year 2018

Table. 3.9 Laos PDR: Socio-Economic Indicators

Indicators	2012	2013	2014	2015	2016	2017	2018
GDP (US$ bn)	9.4	11.2	11.7	12.4	14.5	4.6	4.7
Real GDP growth (%)	8	8.5	7.5	7.4	6.8	6.7	6.5
Consumer price inflation (avg, %)	4.3	6.4	4.1	1.3	1.5	3	2.8
Population (mn)	6.5	6.6	6.7	6.8	6.9	-	-
Merchandise exports fob (US$ bn)	2.3	2.3	2.7	2.8	2.7	2.9	3
Merchandise imports fob (US$ bn)	3.1	3	4.3	5.2	5.5	5.9	6.1
Total int'l reserves (US$ mn)	799	722	875	1,043	925	-	-
Avg Exchange rate (K: US$)	8,008	7,860	8,049	8,148	8,121	8,203	8,275
Life Expectancy at Birth	53.6	56.2	58.9	61.8	66.4	66.7	67
GNI Per capita(2011 PPP$)	2,044	2,416	3,059	3,972	5,523	5,822	6,070
Mean Schooling in Years	3.6	3.9	4.2	4.6	5.1	5.2	5.2
HDI Score	0.428	0.466	0.506	0.546	0.593	0.598	0.601

Source: World Development Report, WB; International Financial Statistics, IMF; Human Development Report, UNDP; Asian Development Outlook, ADB; Various Issues

with an unemployment rate of 1.5%. Laos as a country lacks adequate infrastructure with limited railway network; however, the country has made progress in rural sanitation. Laos PDR had the fourth largest GDP per capita in Indo China during 2018, after Malaysia Singapore, and Thailand. Laos stood at 137th place in terms of Human Development Index (HDI) in the year 2017, indicating medium development. The tourism sector had seen rapid growth from the number of tourists travelling to the country has gone up from 80,000 in 1990 to 1.8 million in 2010. Contribution of the Tourism sector to GNP was around 680 million US Dollars in 2010 and anticipated to reach 1.6 billion US dollars by 2020. Major exports of the country were wood, electricity, coffee, edible fruits, beverages, ores, tin and copper and imports include vehicles, fuel, machinery equipment, iron and steel, and consumer goods. Country major export partners were China, Thailand, Vietnam, India, and Japan and import sources being Thailand, China, Vietnam, South Korea, Japan, and Indonesia during the year 2017.

3.5.8 Brunei Darussalam

Brunei, being among smaller countries, boasts of high living standards because of abundant gas and oil resources. Brunei's head of state "Sultan Hassanal Bolkiah", has abundant private riches and their population, which is made up mostly of ethnic Malay origin enjoy generous state handouts, and they do not pay any taxes. Brunei was under the protection of the British since 1888 and preferred to remain so Malaysia in 1963. Full independence came in 1984. The country's population is 423,000 with an area of 5765 sq km. The 65% of the population comprises of ethnic Malays and 10% Chinese and others, mostly English speaking and well-educated people.

Chart 3.10 Brunei Darussalam

Brunei's political system is Islamic monarchy and currently governed by the penal code under Sharia law. Brunei has joined "Asia-Pacific Economic Cooperation Forum" (APEC) in 1989 and hosted the "APEC Economic Leaders' Meeting" in 2000 and "ASEAN Regional Forum" in 2002. Brunei has strong relations with Singapore and the Philippines. Brunei has hosted the "ASEAN summit" in 2013. The country had converted to the industrialized economy between 1990 to 2000. "International Monetary Fund" (IMF) ranked Brunei 5th in the world by GDP per capita at purchasing power parity (US$32.91 billion). At the official exchange rate, its GDP stands at US$11.97 billion. GDP per capita is US$26939 (2017 estimates).

The oil and gas sectors, which were major sectors of Brunei, have fallen during 2016 and resulted reduction

Table. 3.10 Brunei Darussalam: Socio-Economic Indicators

Indicators	2012	2013	2014	2015	2016	2017	2018
GDP (US$ bn)	19	18.1	17.1	12.9	11.2	-	-
Real GDP growth (%)	0.9	-2.1	-2.3	-0.6	-2.5	0.5	1.4
Consumer price inflation (avg, %)	0.5	0.4	-0.2	-0.4	-0.7	-0.1	0.3
Population (mn)	0.4	0.4	0.4	0.4	0.4	0.4	0.4
Merchandise exports fob (US$ bn)*	13	11.4	10.5	6.4	5	-	-
Merchandise imports fob (US$ bn)*	3.6	3.6	3.6	3.2	3.1	-	-
Total int'l reserves (US$ bn)*	3.3	3.4	3.5	3.2	3.3	-	-
Avg exchange rate (Br$: US$)	1.25	1.25	1.27	1.37	1.38	1.39	1.41
Life Expectancy at Birth	72.9	74.1	75.2	76.3	77	77.2	77.4
GNI Per capita(2011 PPP$)	86,577	82,489	83,411	80,390	78,611	76,870	76,427
Mean Schooling in Years	8.1	8.3	8.5	8.8	9	9.1	9.1
HDI Score	0.805	0.819	0.838	0.842	0.852	0.852	0.853

Source: World Development Report, WB; International Financial Statistics, IMF; Human Development Report, UNDP; Asian Development Outlook, ADB; Various Issues

in Brunei's GDP by 2.5%, apart from resulting in a reduction in investments. The absolute GDP of Brunei during this time reduced from US$12.9 billion in 2015 to US$11.2 billion in 2016. The per capita income was US$28000, and the life expectancy was 77.4 years during 2018., and there seems to be an improvement in the mean schooling of years which was 8.1 years during 2012 and 9.1 years during the year 2018. The Sultanate is ranked 39th out of 189 countries and territories, moving up one place. The HDI score, which was 0.805 during the year 2012 increased to 0.853 during the year 2018. FDI in Brunei has gone up from BND 573 billion in 2012 to BND 1080 in 2012, and then it decreased to BND -206 billion in 2016, again reached to BND 635 billion. Crude oil production constitutes 65% of Brunei's GDP, and production of natural gas constitutes 95% of Brunei's exports. The imports of Brunei were machinery, mineral resources, transport equipment, iron and steel, agricultural products, livestock, food supplements, and electrical machinery. The country exports mineral fuels, machinery, miscellaneous chemicals, organic chemicals, and electricals. The top 5 export partners were Japan, South Korea, India, Thailand, and Singapore as per 2017 and import sources were Malaysia, Singapore, China, USA, Japan, and Thailand.

3.5.9 Cambodia

Although Cambodia gained independence in 1953, various internal struggles, wars and genocides and factional fighting lead to the governance by United Nations for a brief period in 1992-93 following which Cambodian People's party came to power in 1997, and finally, some political stability is achieved by multi-party democracy under a constitutional monarchy. The country spread over 181,035 sq km, with a GDP of 22.25 US$ billion.

Chart 3.11 Cambodia

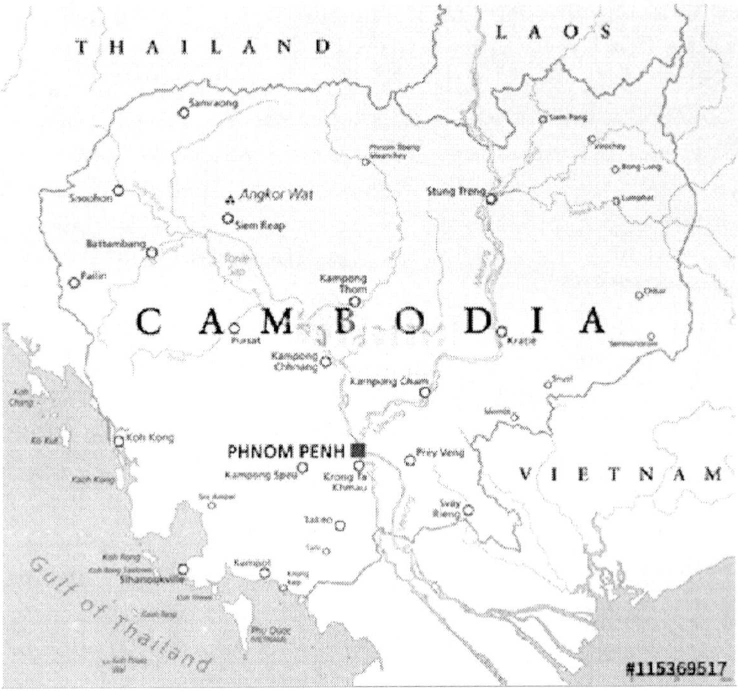

Cambodia was regarded as "low middle-income country" by the "World Bank" in 2016. Cambodia has seen a growth of about 8% per annum during the last 10 years, mainly from sectors such as "Tourism, garments, construction, and real estate". Textile exports occupied a large part of its exports (68% in 2017). Despite the efforts made by government and assistance by IMF and World Bank, the country remains the poorest among the region with a high rate of corruption, limited human resources, high inequalities in income, poverty (17.7% below the poverty line) and unemployment. The HDI rank of Cambodia is 146th in the medium range group with an HDI score of 0582. GDP in 2017 is US$22.25 billion, and GDP per capita is US$1269. The share of agriculture

Table. 3.11 Cambodia: Socio-Economic Indicators

Indicators	2012	2013	2014	2015	2016	2017	2018
GDP (US$ bn)	14	15.4	16.8	18	20	21.3	23.3
Real GDP growth (%)	7.3	7.5	7.1	7	6.8	7	7.2
Consumer price inflation (avg, %)	2.9	2.9	3.9	1.2	3	4	4.2
Population (mn)	14.8	15.1	15.3	15.6	15.8	16.1	16.3
Merchandise exports fob (US$ mn)	5,664	6,565	7,445	8,453	9,233	10,281	11,268
Merchandise imports fob (US$ mn)	8,181	9,794	10,669	11,920	12,648	13,980	15,554
Total int'l reserves (US$ mn)	4,938	4,995	6,106	7,376	9,122a	9,793	9,695
Avg exchange rate (CR : US$)	4,033	4,027	4,038	4,068	4,059	4,083	4,116
Life Expectancy at Birth	55.2	58.4	63.1	66.6	68.6	69	69.3
GNI Per capita(2011 PPP$)	2.7	3	3.2	3.5	4.4	4.7	4.8
Mean Schooling in Years	1,084	1,347	1,889	2,410	3,086	3,246	3,413
HDI Score	0.387	0.42	0.49	0.532	0.571	0.576	0.582

Source: World Development Report, WB; International Financial Statistics, IMF; Human Development Report, UNDP; Asian Development Outlook, ADB; Various Issues

remains 25.3 %, industry 32.8 per cent, and services sector contribution is at 41.9 per cent. The principal exports of the country are "clothing, timber, rubber, rice, fish, tobacco and footwear and imports machinery, motor vehicles, cigarettes, gold, manufacturing items".

3.5.10 Myanmar

Under British rule for more than a century, Burma got independence in 1948. However, there were many ethnic group conflicts throughout post-colonial history until 1962 when the country came under military rule. Following several civil wars internal strife, democratic reforms started in 2011 and culminated in the first elected non-military government in 2015, thus leading to a democratic form of government. Relations with western countries were not that good during military rule; however, after the democratic reforms have started, the USA and UK have lifted sanctions. Myanmar is a member of ASEAN since 1997.

Chart 3.12 Myanmar

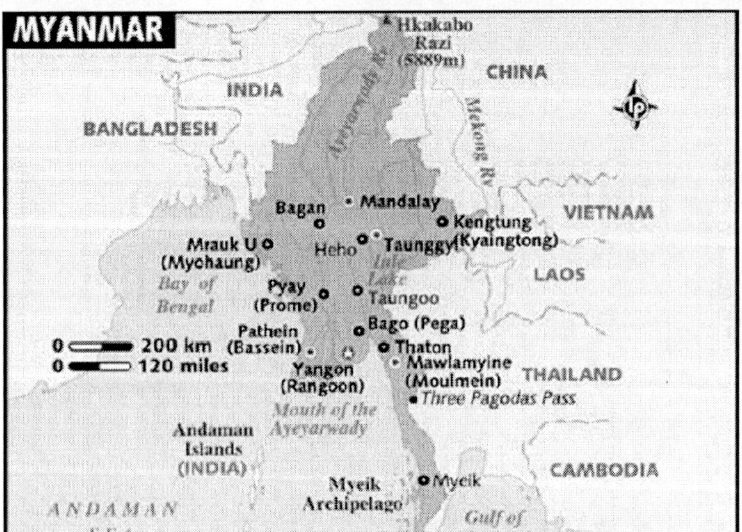

Table. 3.12: Myanmar. Socio-Economic Indicators

Indicators	2012	2013	2014	2015	2016	2017	2018
GDP (US$ bn)	61	62.1	66.3	62.6	65.8	68.5	73.9
Real GDP growth (%)	7.3	8.4	8	7.3	6.4	7.2	6.7
Consumer price inflation (avg, %)	1.5	5.5	5.5	10.8	7	8.4	8.2
Population (mn)	51	51.4	51.9	52.4	52.9	53.4	53.9
Merchandise exports fob (US$ bn)	8.2	9.4	10	9.7	9.1	10.1	10.9
Merchandise imports fob (US$ bn)	7.6	9.5	11.9	13.7	12.8	15.3	16.9
Total int'l reserves (US$ bn)	7	8.6	2	3.8	4.6	5	5.6
Avg exchange rate (Kt: US$)	641	934	984	1,163	1,235	1,362	1,438
Life Expectancy at Birth	60.5	62.1	63.6	65.2	66.5	66.6	66.7
GNI Per capita(2011 PPP$)	959	1,300	2,264	3,717	5,039	5,282	5,567
Mean Schooling in Years	2.7	3.1	3.6	4.1	4.9	4.9	4.9
HDI Score	0.398	0.431	0.477	0.53	0.569	0.574	0.578

Source: World Development Report, WB; International Financial Statistics, IMF; Human Development Report, UNDP: Asian Development Outlook, ADB; Various Issues

It occupies a land area of 676,578 km^2, population of Myanmar consist of about 135 distinct ethnic groups out of which the majority Bamar is highest with 68% followed by 10% of Shan and other groups. Close to 50% of the population is under the poverty line, and the country also suffers from refugees, stateless persons, human trafficking and illicit drugs, etc.

Table 3.12 presents the socio-economic profile of Myanmar, the Gross Domestic Product (PPP) is US$ 73bn, with an unemployment rate of 4% and Gross National Savings were 16 % of the GDP in 2018. The GNI per capita, which is 959 US$ rose to 5,567 US$ from the year 2012 to 2018. There was a significant improvement with the Human Development Indicator scores, which rose from 0.398 in the year 2012 to 0.578 in the year 2018. The country ranks 145 out of the 189 countries in HDI ranking the latest ranks.

Agriculture constitutes 24.8% of GDP and Industry about 35.4% which consists of "Agricultural processing, Wood and wood products, metals such as copper, tin, tungsten and iron, cement and construction materials", etc. Exports primarily consist of "natural gas, wooden products, pulses and beans, fish, rice, clothing, minerals, jade, and Gems". The country imports fertilizers, plastics, petroleum products, machinery, edible oil, transport equipment and fabric. The service sector accounted for 39.9% in GDP. The key partners for export are China, Thailand, Japan, India, and South Korea, and the top five primary sources of imports include China, Singapore, Thailand, Saudi Arabia, and Malaysia.

3.5.11 Vietnam

Vietnam was a French colony from 1884 to 1954, and after that got divided into South and North Vietnam. The conflict its colonisers lead to the Vietnam War, which started in 1965 and ended in 1975 with North Vietnam taking over South Vietnam and a reunification happened. After reunification also country made little progress for ten years but later from 1984 onwards the economy has opened to build relations with the external world following economic reforms. Table 3.13 presents the Socio-economic profile of Vietnam.

Chart 3.13 Vietnam

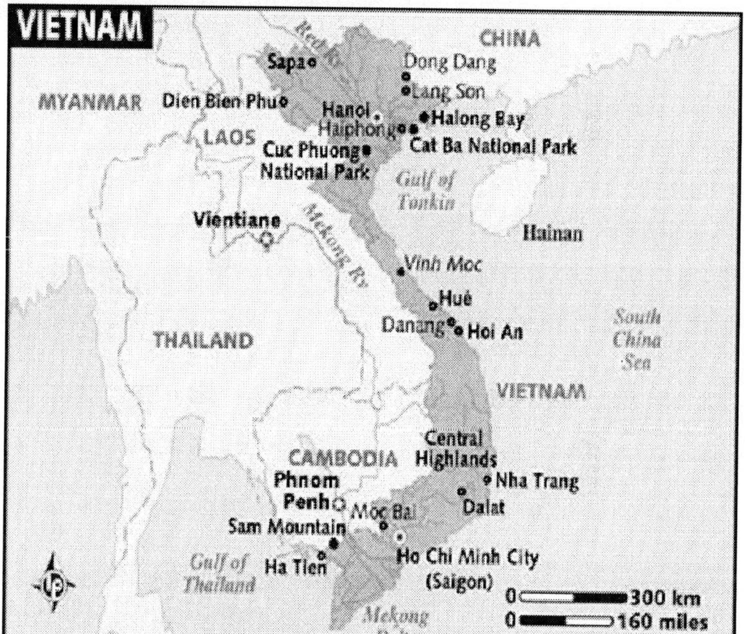

Vietnam's land area is a total of 331,212 square kilometres and GDP stands at US$205 billion in 2017, with GDP per capita of US$2170. The GNI per capita, which was US$1,936 in the year 2012, showed an improvement and rose to 5,859 by the year 2018. The HDI score, which was 0.529 in the year 2012 rose to 0.694 by the year 2018. The country stands at 116 HDI ranking among the 189 countries. The majority of the

Table. 3.13: Vietnam. Socio-Economic Indicators

Indicators	2012	2013	2014	2015	2016	2017	2018
GDP (US$ bn)	155.6	170.5	185.8	191.4	201.4	213.6	222.3
Real GDP growth (%)	5.2	5.4	6	6.7	6.2	6.3	6.5
Consumer price inflation (avg., %)	9.1	6.6	4.1	1.7	2.7	3.4	3.8
Population (mn)	90.5	91.5	92.5	93.6	94.6	95.5	96.5
Merchandise exports fob (US$ bn)	104.8	123.3	138.1	154.7	162.6	191.1	212.2
Merchandise imports fob (US$ bn)	77.4	97.4	104.7	123.4	138.6	163.9	192.7
Total int'l reserves (US$ bn)	26.1	26.3	34.6	28.6	36.9	39.4	38.8
Avg exchange rate (D: US$)	20,859	21,017	21,189	21,958	20,555	22,928	24,136
Life Expectancy at Birth	72	73.3	74.3	75.1	76.1	76.3	76.5
GNI Per capita(2011 PPP$)	1,936	2,712	3,348	4,241	5,263	5,589	5,859
Mean Schooling in Years	4.6	5.4	6.4	7.5	8	8.1	8.2
HDI Score	0.529	0.579	0.616	0.654	0.684	0.689	0.694

Source: World Development Report, WB; International Financial Statistics, IMF; Human Development Report, UNDP; Asian Development Outlook, ADB; Various Issues

population consists of 87% of Kings (local Vietnamese), and the rest of the population is made up of people from over 50 ethnic groups. Since 1986, Vietnam has a stable political system to support fast-paced economic growth. The service sector is predominant in the economy with 41.3%, followed by Industry at 32.7% and agriculture at 15.9%. Among the industries, the notable are "food processing, garments, shoes, machine-building, mining, coal, cement, fertilizer, glass, tires, oil, and mobile phones". The rate of unemployment is 7%, and the Gross National Savings was at 28%. From 2012 to 2016, Vietnam's total exports and imports have increased at a CAGR of 12.7%.

Exports have gone up from US$104.8 billion by more than double to US$212.2 billion. Similarly, imports also have gone up from 77.4 billion US dollars to 192.7 billion US dollars. "United States, China, Japan, and South Korea" are major export partners and Vietnam exports "clothes, shoes, electronics, seafood, crude oil, rice, coffee, wooden products and machinery", while it imports "machinery &equipment, petroleum products, steel, raw materials for clothing and shoes, electronics, plastics, and automobiles". The primary import sources are "China, South Korea, Japan, USA, and Thailand".

3.6 NEW STRATEGY TOWARDS ASEAN: LOOK EAST POLICY

Few member states of ASEAN and India have common sea or land border, thus have a natural disposition to become trade partners. Historically, India and countries of ASEAN have used silk route, and now they use routes which are technology-oriented. "Look East Policy" of India is mainly directed to develop relations with ASEAN countries both for trade and social aspects. Indian Government has placed further emphasis on this policy and re-christened as "Act East Policy". From being sectoral dialogue partner to full dialogue partner, India has proceeded with a strategic partnership with ASEAN then onwards. The partnership over the years has seen expansion in trade and intensification of economic linkages, and by 2017, the partnership reached a milestone of 25 years as dialogue partnership and 15 years as Summit partnership

India and ASEAN together present one of the biggest commercial blocs, having 185 crores people, a quarter of world population and a total GDP of US$3.8 trillion. They have been establishing cooperation in various fields and implementing a different kind of projects in "agriculture, space, science and technology, environment and climate change, human resource development, capacity building, new and renewable energy, tourism, people-to-people contacts, and connectivity" (Exim Bank, 2018), and so far projects worth US$48 million were proposed, and these are under implementation. Some of the projects were enumerated below.

- "Space Project" to establish a station for "tracking, data reception/data processing in Ho Chi Minh City, Vietnam;"
- Project to upgrade "telemetry tracking and command station in Biak, Indonesia";
- Project to set up "'centres of excellence in software development & training in 'CLMV' countries";
- Project to set up e-Network for the facilitation of telemedicine and tele-education in CLMV countries. (Exim Bank, 2018)

3.7 "ASEAN-INDIA COMPREHENSIVE ECONOMIC COOPERATION AGREEMENT"

India and ASEAN have signed "The ASEAN - India Framework Agreement on Comprehensive Economic Cooperation" (CECA) in Indonesia during October 200 to institutionalize a plan co-operation in coming years. There are two aspects to this agreement, as given below.

- "Trade-in Goods Agreement"
- "Trade-in Services and Investment Agreement"

The above two agreements are the basis of "ASEAN-India Free Trade Area" (AIFTA)". Both the regions have signed "The ASEAN-India Trade in Goods Agreement" after deliberations for six years in 2009, and it got implemented from January 1, 2010. They also signed "The ASEAN-India Agreement on Investment and Trade in Services" in November 2014, which got implemented from July 1, 2015.

3.7.1 "Trade in Goods Agreement"

"The ASEAN-India Agreement on Trade in Goods" got implemented on different dates with different groups of ASEAN member states. "Malaysia, Singapore, Thailand, Vietnam, Myanmar, Indonesia, Brunei" joined the agreement on different dates from January to November 2010, followed by "Lao PDR, Philippines, Cambodia" during 2011. Similarly, the timelines for implementation of tariff reductions/elimination also have been drawn. For commodities under "normal track 1 and 2, sensitive track, special products and highly sensitive track", these tariff changes will be implemented for five countries "Singapore, Thailand, Indonesia, Malaysia, Vietnam" in 2019, followed by the Philippines in 2022, and for CLMV countries in 2024.

3.7.2 "Trade in Services & Investment Agreement"

India and ASEAN have signed "The ASEAN-India Trade in Services Agreement" during November 2014, and it has been implemented from July 2015. The agreement contained articles that include "transparency, domestic regulations, recognition, market access, and national treatment, increasing participation of developing countries, joint committee on services, review, dispute settlement and denial of benefits" (Exim Bank, 2018) The agreement's primary purpose was to uphold the interest of the investors, especially to treat the investors equally and with legitimate remuneration.

"The ASEAN-India Trade in Services and Investment Agreement" encompasses the "General Agreement on Trade in Services" (GATS) along with obligations under which service supplies are committed. Individual member states of ASEAN agreed on the obligations and commitments. India and the ASEAN Member countries were parties to "General Agreement of Trades in Services" (GATS) and had commitments with regards to modes of supply and various services as per norms of "World Trade Organisation"(WTO).

3.7.3 "Regional Comprehensive Economic Partnership (RCEP) Agreement"

The AIFTA has come into implementation from July 2015 and India participated actively in the "Regional Comprehensive Economic Partnership" deliberations, to make it a most promising regional trading agreement. "Regional Comprehensive Economic Partnership" (RCEP) is an agreement for the establishment of the free trade agreement (FTA) among ASEAN and other Free Trade Agreement partners of ASEAN such as "Australia, China, India, Japan, South Korea and New Zealand". RCEP discussions started in November 2012, at the "ASEAN Summit" in Cambodia. Since then, there were several detailed discussions held to conclude this multi-party agreement. During July 2017, an "RCEP Trade Negotiating Committee" meeting took place in Hyderabad, India. The delegates from participating countries have agreed to work in close coordination for achieving the objectives of the agreement.

3.7.4 "Mekong-Ganga Cooperation"

"The Mekong-Ganga Cooperation (MGC)", formed in November 2000 in Lao PDR– India and five countries of ASEAN namely, "Thailand, Cambodia, Lao PDR, Myanmar, and Vietnam" – to cooperate and assist each other in the fields of "tourism, education, culture, transport and communication". The two rivers "Ganga and Mekong" were valued rivers for centuries the effort is to increase people to people communication and contacts residing in the river basins of these two rivers. The MGC also signifies centuries-old cultural and commercial ties among its member nations. Participants of the 8th "Mekong Ganga Cooperation Ministerial Meeting" occurred in 2017 in the Philippines, have expressed the need to find ways improve economic ties and to exploit business opportunities between India and the countries along Mekong river.

3.7.5 "India's Act East Policy"

"The Look East Policy" has been propounded by India to address economic slowdown it was facing. "The Look East Policy" eventually became "Act East Policy" that is supposed to be an action-oriented approach towards building relations with Asian countries. Some of the decisive moves of this policy include a "Project Development Fund" with Rs.500 Crores funding for catalyzing some of the projects Indian companies are involved in CLMV countries. There was also "Market Access Initiative" which was promoted by Ministry of Commerce and Industries, which funded about 14 events in 2016-2017 alone, to promote Indian projects in ASEAN member states.

Few more agreements were signed between ASEAN as given below:

- "Plan of Action to Implement the ASEAN-INDIA Partnership for Peace, Progress and Shared Prosperity" (2016- 2020);
- "Treaty of Amity and Cooperation in Southeast Asia"
- "ASEAN - India Joint Declaration for Cooperation to Combat International Terrorism, Bali, Indonesia, October 2003"

3.7.6 "Plan of Action to Implement the ASEAN-INDIA Partnership for Peace, Progress and Shared Prosperity (2016-2020)"

In order to deepen the cooperation between India and ASEAN both the partners have signed the "ASEAN-India Partnership for Peace, Progress and Shared Prosperity", at the time of 3rd "ASEAN-India Summit" during November 2004. The participants have approved the plan of action and decided to take it forward towards implementation subsequently at the "ASEAN Post Ministerial Conference" during August 2015 in Malaysia. "The POA 2016-2020 comprises three broad areas, namely the political and security cooperation; economic cooperation; and socio-cultural cooperation. This POA lays out the priorities and measures to be undertaken by both sides to deepen further and enhance their political-security, economic and socio-cultural ties as well as to realize the full potential of the ASEAN-India strategic partnership in all areas which are of common interests to both the sides".(Asean.org)

3.8 CONCLUSION

India has realized and experienced the potential of trading with the ASEAN regional group and is keen to further intensify the bilateral trading regime with the group for a better future for both sides. Both sides realized that there is enough room for expanding and strengthening the cooperation, as there is much that is so much commonality between India's and the ASEAN socio-economic goals. The possibilities for functional cooperation between India and ASEAN are limitless, which need to be materialized and implemented. The next chapter would analyze trade between India and ASEAN and the related trends.

4

India's Trade with the ASEAN: An Analysis

ASEAN regional block has seen remarkable economic and social progress for the past five decades, enhanced intra-ASEAN cooperation and reduced gaps in development among countries in the ASEAN region. ASEAN-10 is regarded as a region of promising potential and has been an attractive destination for business, trade, and investment. The ASEAN economy has expanded over 100 fold with a combined "GDP of US$ 2.55 trillion in 2016, with a share of 6.2 per cent in the world GDP (based on US$ at PPP). In 2016, the combined GDP of ASEAN, as a single economy, placed it as the sixth-largest in the world and the third-largest in Asia", (Exim Bank, 2018)

Indian Economy is gaining prominence as 7th largest globally concerning GDP in 2016. It also has diverse sectors such as agriculture which adopted modern methods, service sector with a different type of services and industrial sector with various industries and product lines. The economy also has grown at 8% in GDP during 2015-16, fastest in previous 5 years as a result of the increase in investments and consumption although the growth had slightly slowed down to 7.1% in 2016-17. India is likely to get further impetus to its economy with initiatives such as GST which has implications to cost of business operations, reduction on logistics costs.

ASEAN and India have improved their economic relations as well as political and diplomatic relations. Although the volumes of investment and trade between India and ASEAN have been a bit lower with the other trade-partners of ASEAN, the volumes in absolute terms have been continually rising. By 2017, the partnership between ASEAN and India has completed 25 years. In this context, this chapter analyses the changing trends of trade between ASEAN regional group and India.

The chapter is presented in seven sections. Section one presents the objectives of the chapter, while section two presents the methodology adopted. Section three analyses the Trade Openness Indicators of India and the ASEAN countries respectively and Indo-ASEAN Trade trends are presented in Section Four, Section five presents intensity (export and import) of India's trade with individual ASEAN nations along with the modified trade intensity indices and Section six, summaries the essential findings of the chapter and the last section gives the conclusion.

4.1. OBJECTIVES

1. To review the degree of trade openness of India and the ASEAN.
2. To observe the intensity of India's trade with ASEAN.
3. To analyze the trade trends of India's trade share with the ASEAN.
4. To examine the volume of India's imports from and exports to the ASEAN market.

4.2. METHODOLOGY

The following methodology has been adopted to appraise the performance of India's trade with ASEAN member states. Initially, through the Trade Openness indicators are used to assess the integration of domestic economies of India and the ASEAN countries with the outside world. In the same section, ASEAN nations exports/imports to India along with "China, Japan, and the USA" as the proportion of World Total Exports/ Imports were also presented. To assess the trade trends between India and the ASEAN, the proportion of India's Export to and Imports from ASEAN nations has been assessed from the year 2000 to 2017. Similarly, the values of the coefficient of variation, correlation, growth rates along with t-ratios and F –Test have been done for India's Exports to and Imports from each of the ASEAN nations over the period taken for study. India's "Export Intensity Index" and "Import Intensity Index" with the ASEAN member states are calculated from 2000 to 2017. Further, the "Modified Intensity Index" is used to estimate the values of trade for the period of study. A brief description of each of the methodologies used is presented here.

4.2.1. "Trade Openness Indicator":

The "Trade Openness Index" (TOI) is a measure, and it is expressed as a TOI for a country as the ratio of its total trade (value of exports and imports added together) to its gross domestic product (GDP).

Trade Openness Indicator of the Country= (Exports + Imports)/ (Gross Domestic Product)

4.2.2. ASEAN's share of trade with Select partner regions

Individual ASEAN nation's percentage trade value (Exports and Imports separately) as a proportion of the value of global trade (separately for Exports and Imports) are calculated and presented for India, China, Japan, and the USA for the period 2009 to 2017. To present a comparative analysis for ASEAN trade with India to that of China, Japan, and the USA who are competing with India.

4.2.3. India's share of trade with ASEAN member nations

India's percentage trade share(exports and Imports separately) are calculated for the years 2000 to 2017, further to strengthen the study, values of the coefficient of variation, correlation, growth rates along with t-ratios & F –Test has been done for India's Exports/Imports separately with each of the ASEAN nations over the period taken for study.

4.2.3.1 Growth Model:

Going by the standard mathematical models, the following formulae are used to find growth rates of different variables such as exports and imports.

$Y_t = a\, e^{b^*t} e^{u}_t$

Which can be written as

$\text{Log } Y_t = \log a + b^*t + u_t$

Exponential Function

In order to estimate the growth rates, the following function is used.

$Y_t = f(t, u_t)$ .... (1)

$Y_t = a\, e^{b^*t} e^{u}_t$ .... (2)

Where Y= Exports / imports

t= time period and

u= the stochastic disturbance term

The above relationship can be rewritten as

$\text{Log } Y_t = \text{Log } a + b^*t + u_t$ .... (3)

This can be estimated by the method of Ordinary Least Square (OLS). Here

$B=(dY/y) / (dt)$ .... (4)

4.2.3.2 Correlation Coefficient

Correlation Coefficient is used to calculate "exponential growth rate". It calculates "proportionate change in 'Y' for a unit change in time". A correlation coefficient is a number which measures whether there is a linear relationship and how strong is the relation between two continuous variables.

The resultant values are between +1 and -1.

Strength of the Correlation: The absolute value of the correlation coefficient indicates the strength of the correlation. Higher the value of correlation, stronger is the relationship between the variables.

1. If the value falls close to -1 or +1, towards the extremes, that means the variables have a perfect linear relationship. In such case, for a given change in one variable is an entirely consistent change in other variable can be seen, and the data points of the variables would fall in on a line. However, we do not find such perfect relationships in reality.
2. If the coefficient's value is zero, that indicates the absence of the linear relationship between the two variables. If one variable increases, the other variable does not tend to either decrease or increase.
3. If the value of the coefficient falls between 0 and +1/-1, the data points do not fall on a line, and the relationship is non-linear. Moreover, as the coefficient's value comes closer to -1 or 1, the strength of correlation increases, and the data points fall on a line.

Correlation Co-efficient: r = •(Xi-X) (Yi-Y) / n

Where sample size is 'n', the correlation coefficient is 'r', the value of the independent variable is 'X', and the value of the dependent variable is 'Y.'

4.2.3.3 *Tests of Significance of the Parameter Estimates*

Since 'a' and 'b' are sample estimates of the parameters, 'a' and 'b' testing is required to find their statistical reliability. Some of the standard tests of significance are the coefficient of Determination, t-test and F-test. A brief explanation of these concepts is given in this section.

t-test

Together with the value of r^2, it is necessary to compute the standard errors of the regression coefficients. Some econometricians report the t-ratios of the estimated coefficients in place of standard errors because this way of presentation makes the testing of hypothesis easier and direct. The t-ratio for 'b' is

$t_b = b \ / \ S.E\ (b)$

Where S.E. (b) = $\sqrt{\ }$ Var (b)

$\sum (X_i - \bar{X})^2$

Var (b) = $\sigma_u^2 /$

Est. Var (b) = $\ _u^2 /$

Where $\ _u^2 =$

Here $\ _u^2$ = an unbiased estimator of the variance of disturbance and n=number of observations.

The t-ratio for '$\hat{a}$' is

$t_a = a /$ S.E. ('$\hat{a}$')

Where S.E. (b) = $\sqrt{\ }$ Var (b)

$$\text{Var (b)} = \sigma_u^2 / \sum (X_i - \overline{X})^2$$

$$\text{Est. Var (b)} = \hat{\sigma}_u^2 / \sum (X_i - \overline{X})^2$$

$$\text{Where } \hat{\sigma}_u^2 = \sum e_i^2 (n-2)$$

If t* < t (the tabulated value of t at (n-2) degrees of freedom), we accept the null hypothesis*, that is, we accept that '$\hat{b}$' is not significant and the regressor time does not seem to explain the variations in Y.

If t* > t (the tabulated value of t at (n-2) degree of freedom), the null hypothesis is rejected, the alternative hypothesis is accepted; that is, '$\hat{b}$' is statistically significant. Thus, the higher the value of t*, the stronger the '$\hat{b}$' statistically significant evidence.

Coefficient of Determination

According to standard statistical analysis tools, "to test whether our fit is best or not, it is necessary to estimate r^2, the coefficient of determination. r^2 measures the proportion of variations in the dependent variable that is explained by variation in the independent variables. This definition is valid only when the particular regression model contains a constant term. If our fit is perfect $\sum e_i^2 = 0$ and $r^2 = 1$, indicating the best fit. At the other extreme $r^2 = 0$, indicating that the estimated regression line is horizontal. Thus, the limits of r^2 are zero and unity.

$$r^2 = 1 - \left(\sum e_i^2\right) / \left(\sum y_i^2\right)$$

Where $\sum e_i^2$ – Unexplained sum of squares,

And $\left(\sum y_i^2\right)$ = Total sum of square (Explained sum of squares $(\hat{b}\sum X_i^2)$ + Unexplained sum of squares)"

4.2.4 Intensity Indices

"Trade Intensity Index (TII)" is employed to observe the pattern of exports and imports between two partner countries. "TII is further divided into Export Intensity Index (XII) and Import Intensity Index (MII)". As given by Kojima (1964) and Drysdale (1969), these indices can be explained as given below. (Kojima, 1964 and Drysdale, 1969).

4.2.4.1 "Export intensity Index

The ratio of the export share of a country/region to the share of world exports to a partner country. XII can be defined as,

$$XII_{ij} = \frac{x_{ij} / X_{iw}}{x_{wj} / X_{ww}}$$

Where x_{ij} is the value of exports of country *i* to country *j*, X_{iw} is the value of the exports of country *i* to the world, x_{wj} is the value of world exports to country *j*, and X_{ww} is the value of world exports. An index value greater than one presents that trade flow between countries is greater than expected, given their importance in world trade."

4.2.4.2 "Import Intensity Index

The ratio of import share of a country/region to the share of world imports going to a partner. MII can be defined as,

$MII_{ij} = M_{ij} / M_{iw} / M_{wj} / M_{ww}$

Where M_{ij} is the value of imports of country *i* to country *j*, M_{iw} is the value of the imports of country *i* to the world, M_{wj} is the value of world imports to country *j*, and M_{ww} is the value of world imports. An index value of greater than one presents higher import intensity between the nations." (Radha Raghuramapatruni, 2012)

The "Export Intensity Index" and the "Import Intensity Index" of India and Select countries of ASEAN were calculated to estimate the Intensity of trade between India and the ASEAN.

4.2.4.3 Modified Trade Intensity Index

"Trade Intensity Index" formula is changed by substituting Exports of "Rest of the World (RoW)" in place of 'Exports of the World' as explained hereunder (Rest of the World exports is equal to as 'Exports of the World' minus Exports of the Country 'i') to derive the "Modified Trade Intensity Index".

" $T'II = (X_{ij}/X_{it})/X'_{wj}/X'_{wt})$

Where X'_{wj} =Rest of the World's exports to country $j = X_{wj} - X_{ij}$ and X'_{wt}=Rest of the World's exports=$X_{wt} - X_{it}$. We define T'_{ij} as modified TII. For countries with an insignificant share in world exports, values of T_{ij} and T'_{ij} will remain almost the same. The difference may be higher for countries with a higher share in world exports." "Values of the index (T_{ij} or T'_{ij}) will be one for expected bilateral trade flow. Share of one country's exports to its partner should be at least equal to the share of world exports to the same partner for expected bilateral trade flow. Otherwise, it means that the country fails to exploit the market in its partner country, and there is scope for expansion of its exports trade in the partner country. An index of more (less) than one indicates a bilateral trade flow that is greater (smaller) than expected, given the partner country's importance in world trade" Radha Raghuramapatruni, (2012).

4.3 TRADE OPENNESS INDICATORS BETWEEN INDIA AND ASEAN

After World War II, Development Economics gained popularity, and greater importance was given to economic growth. The assumption was that manufacturing would lead to the material wealth of economies and the living standards would improve, but with the success of Japanese economy during 1970-80s following the East Asian Economic miracle growth story, economists and development agencies now advocate trade openness, instead of protection, import-substitution for the economy's growth. Following the economist Clark (1997) that developing economies have got successful as they embraced extrovert and open trade policies instead of protectionist and price manipulating, in-ward looking import-substitution policies. In this background, before starting the analyses of India's trade with the ASEAN, a review on the Trade Openness Indicators of India along with each of the ASEAN-10 members is calculated and presented in the Table. 4.1. Which would help in understanding the integration of domestic economies with the external world, which plays a crucial role in international trade.

The East Asian Economies were the main beneficiaries of changes in economic policies after world war due to globalization since they have opened their economies and taken up export-led growth strategies and supplied

Table. 4.1 Trade Openness Indicator of India and the ASEAN Nations (2000-2017)

Year	India	Singapore	Indonesia	Malaysia	Philippine	Thailand	Laos PDR	Brunei Da	Cambodia	Vietnam	Mynamar	ASEAN 10
2000	19.70108	284.1794		82.9864	92.6965	103.5555	55.0680	75.1986	90.6785	96.6160	38.9080	147.2457
2001	13.98088	266.2743		76.3782	37.9484	105.5139	53.0211	77.1752	90.0192	96.0737	69.7841	129.3984
2002	20.19348	262.7939		76.4344	93.7830	98.8474	45.1407	81.0544	98.8809	103.8607	68.3730	129.1658
2003	21.26895	305.2689	57.0506	72.4649	93.9204	102.5393	39.2327	78.9669	100.2774	114.7666	37.5527	143.3677
2004	24.44937	325.9966	51.8443	80.2605	93.8839	110.2739	45.3269	74.1389	112.3225	118.0408	37.2087	150.0385
2005	29.06745	337.2281	59.2795	79.6660	38.0359	121.0207	52.8174	73.1500	111.6351	120.0441	41.1653	150.9562
2006	31.63123	345.4224	50.5423	80.3054	33.0483	116.5657	54.7213	73.1178	116.4505	127.7856	42.3615	153.5639
2007	35.63525	312.5124	53.4251	76.2268	72.6174	111.7478	47.1790	71.9556	110.3980	148.5026	40.8572	132.3957
2008	42.1421	342.2736	59.2635	68.3969	53.0733	122.5200	47.1480	80.5433	108.4551	145.9245	32.2945	157.5450
2009	30.91543	267.984	49.1425	62.4268	50.0422	101.5693	45.0333	81.1356	96.4933	125.0026	28.9730	112.8438
2010	33.74877	280.2885	42.0884	67.9478	55.0945	110.2964	55.6387	83.4994	106.2495	139.2869	27.0902	117.2496
2011	42.09384	281.2987	39.6294	66.0191	49.9671	121.7307	56.9802	86.8753	124.8567	151.3312	30.4400	131.3077
2012	43.02355	272.5461	37.2205	65.2803	46.9622	120.2869	56.6573	87.0014	136.5021	146.8369	30.2662	135.4857
2013	42.01106	258.9214	36.1506	67.1654	45.0284	113.8852	49.5447	83.2391	106.4097	154.9260	38.7064	135.2523
2014	33.63017	251.6756	38.9150	65.1644	45.9241	111.9771	58.5035	82.5101	104.5292	160.4567	42.2094	124.0654
2015	31.62172	216.7478	16.5704	63.2655	45.6754	104.4446	63.7032	74.0950	114.7544	171.2989	47.5552	108.0446
2016	27.71461	212.1415	14.5480	60.8254	48.1927	100.6479	58.6772	70.5951	117.0275	174.5351	41.5174	99.3845
2017	30.37808	240.1583	15.3770	67.2721	49.0512	106.1353	60.4502	68.0269	123.7532	197.3049	41.1784	104.2840
Average	31.0117	281.3173	42.7366	71.0270	56.9411	110.1971	52.4911	77.9059	109.4274	138.2000	40.9132	131.2006

Sources: Author's Calculations based unctad.com

to the expanding import needs of manufactured products by the western countries. This could be viewed from the Trade Openness Indicator values of ASEAN-10. The initial Trade Openness indicator value during the year 2000 is 147.250, and for the year 2017, this was 104.284 due to the declining values of exports and imports of the member countries owing to the US subprime crisis of 2007-2008. The indicator which was experiencing an upward trend till the year 2008 (157.545) thereafter started a declining trend after that, gradually increased after that since the year 2011 (131.308), again reached a two-digit level figure value with 99.385 for the year 2016 and remained at 104.284 for the year 2017 because of the economic slowdown in the global markets. Other individual economies also exhibited the same trend. Singapore whose Trade Openness Indicators values are greater than the ASEAN as a whole owing to the huge amount of the transit trade of the country. The average Trade Openness indicator of the country is at 281.317. Singapore strategic economic planning of 1991, the government has taken up several resolute steps to advance, making its economy the World leader in the newly industrialized nations. Though the crisis of 2007-08 affected the economy with a decline in exports and imports but the economy regained back, which could be observed in the Trade Openness indicator values of Singapore. Indonesia, like many other neighbouring countries, it has initiated the reforms in its export policies before taking up liberalization of imports, and this resulted in what was known to be a distortion in the policy. The deregulation measures adopted by Indonesia earlier did not help much because of the Non-Tariff barriers (NTBs) that have impacted a major portion of their imports. This could be viewed with the low values of Trade Openness Indicators when compared to the other ASEAN 10, the Trade Openness Indicator value which was 57.051 during the year 2003 received a setback during the crisis period of 2007-08 and later reduced drastically to 15.377 in the year 2017 where the country also faced natural calamities during the two consecutive years. Many economists have described Malaysia as a fast-growing economy in the East. The country adopted the liberalizing regime since 1981 through a series of pronouncements and reforms, including privatization of state utilities, changes in its tax administration whereby it is done through cuts indirect and corporate taxes. This could be observed in the value of Trade Openness indicator value ratio, which was 82.986 declines to 68.399 post-crisis and reduces to 67.272 during the period 2017. The average ratio of Malaysia is 71.027. The trade openness indicators for the Philippines is 92.697 for the year 2000, and this has declined to 49.051 during the year 2016, and the average lies at 66.941. The Philippine economic development was close to Japan during the period 1960s, but after it joined WTO in 1995, the country opened up to international economy with its internal political economy not prepared for, underdeveloped resulting in the slow economic growth of the economy. The Thai economy is the economy that collapsed because of the 1997 Asian financial crisis. However, the revival of the economy was quick and within 10 years period of time if it could regain back the GDP of 1996. Initially, the Trade Openness Indicator (TOI) was 103.556 for the year 2000, and there was a significant increase till the year 2008 with 122.520 value and decline to 106.135 during the year 2017. The average value of the index is 110.197. Laos PDR made modest improvements in international integration by the year 1997, when it had opened its economy considerably. The value of TOI which was 55.063 in the year 2000 and this has reduced to 47.179 in the year 2007 and finally was at 60.450 by the year 2017. The average Trade Openness Indicator (TOI) rests at 52.491. Brunei's concern was that the assimilation in to the global economy would impact social cohesion in the country adversely, but the country has taken steps to become a more prominent player in "Asia Pacific Economic Cooperation" (APEC) meetings, the initial period the TOI rests at 75.200, and this has reduced during the 2008 crisis and finally ended with 68.027. The average TOI value is 77.906. Cambodia follows market economy and open trade system and it has seen speedy progress in its economy during last decade. Initially the value of Trade Openness indicator (TOI) is 90.616 and by the year 2008 this was at 108.455 and gradually increased to 123.753 which could be due to the open trade system followed by the country. Vietnam was part of CARICOM during the early 1990s, and it was largely dependent on the trade with the Soviet Union. After the dissolution of the CARICOM since the original trading partners were lost, Vietnam had to go for liberalization of its trade and devaluation of its exchange rate for increasing exports. The Initial Period of 2000 the exchange rate is 96.616 and slowly rose to 145.925 during the year 2008 and later received a set-back post-crisis of 2008 but with the export promotion measures taken the economy revived with an increase in the volume of trade and GDP values where the TOI indicator could be seen at 197.305. Myanmar economy is seen as the lease free in Asia as largely tied with North Korea. Foreign investments primarily coming from China, Singapore, South Korea, India and Thailand the year 200 the TOI indicator is at 38.903, and this rose to 40.857 in the year 2007 and later reduced to 41.178 by the year 2017. The average TOI indicator rests at 40.913. Compared with East Asian countries, the Trade Openness Indicator of India is low. The average TOI indicator for India is at 31.012, which is least compared with the other Asian partners. For the initial period, the TOI indicator is at 19.701, and there was a gradual increase till the year 2008 which is at 42.142 and there was a significant increase by the year 2017 which is at 30.378, except for the years 2014 (31.622) and 2015 (31.622). The gradual increase in the integration of the economy through series of policy implementations and acts and trade liberalization measures are taken up to liberalize the economy, and this could also be seen in the country ease of doing business index moving up to 77th position in the year 2019. However, the Trade Openness indicators present the more integration and strength of the Asian countries in comparison to India during the period taken for the study and the countries are gradually liberalizing their trade regime to integrate with the world economy.

4.4 ASEAN TRADE WITH INDIA

The ASEAN economy has grown over time, and it signifies the importance of international trade, helping the Asian region. Total trade of ASEAN constitutes 7.1% of the total trade of the world, and it stands fourth among the trading blocks in the world, next to the European Union, USA and China. Over the last 50 years, the proportion of ASEAN in global has increased more than three times, reaching 7.2 per cent in the year 2016, up from 2 per cent in the year 1967. Meanwhile, the proportion of ASEAN in global imports too increased phenomenally to reach 6.6% in the year 2016, up from 2.3 per cent in 1967. In the last ten years, total trade has increased from US$ 1.6 trillion in the year 2007 to US$ 2.3 trillion in the year 2016, and a steep decline in 2009, during the period of world financial crisis, later followed by slow growth in 2015 coinciding with slow-down in global trade. Exports of ASEAN nations to India as a percentage of World Exports is presented in Table. 4.2. A comparison with China, Japan and the USA were made to analyze the relative position of India for the period 2009 to 2017. Also, ASEAN imports from India and comparison with China, Japan and the USA are presented in Table. 4.3.

4.4.1 ASEAN Nations Exports to India as a Percentage of Total World Exports

A trend of gradual decrease of ASEAN nation's exports to India could be observed from the Table 4.2 since 2000 to 2009 and it started gradually rising after 2009 to 2017 in the light of 2009 being the post-recovery period for the world along with India and the ASEAN nations from the subprime crisis, whereas ASEAN exports to China has seen continuous rise from the year 2000 to 2017 growing more than three times. In the year 2009 the percentage export share of ASEAN to India is 3.28 % for the same period it is 10.05 with China and 9.63 with Japan and 10.12 with the USA. Initially, India was ASEAN's primary destination for exports after Japan and the USA but lost its position to China over the years. Similarly, ASEAN's exports to Japan have reduced by 50% from the year 2000 to 2017 and exports to the USA also reduced slightly. As the volume of trade between ASEAN and the World is significant, India continued to be an essential player in the ASEAN's market although less compared to China, Japan and the USA. India's exports to ASEAN during the pre-AIFTA period (2003-2009) was growing at CAGR of 23.39 %, and imports were growing at a CAGR of 23.71%. At the same time, the trade deficit of India also has grown by 24.69% from US$ 1.62 billion to US$ 6.07 billion.

When the exports of the individual nation as percentage of world exports to ASEAN nations were analyzed Indonesia has the highest share for the year 2017 with 8.34% of the overall exports are directed towards India among its total exports, followed by Brunei Darussalam with 4.75% of its exports directed towards India, followed by Myanmar 4.71%, Lao PDR 4.48 %, Malaysia 3.69%, Singapore (2.87%), Thailand (2.74%), Vietnam (1.76%), Philippines (08.80%) and Cambodia with

Table 4.2 ASEAN Nations Exports to India as a Percentage of Total World Exports

		[illegible]	[illegible]	[illegible]	[illegible]	[illegible]	[illegible]	[illegible]	[illegible]	[illegible]	[illegible]	[illegible]	[illegible]	[illegible]	[illegible]	[illegible]	[illegible]	[illegible]	[illegible]
ASEAN	India	[illegible]	[illegible]	[illegible]	[illegible]	[illegible]	[illegible]	[illegible]	[illegible]	[illegible]	[illegible]	[illegible]	[illegible]	[illegible]	[illegible]	[illegible]	[illegible]	[illegible]	[illegible]
	China	[illegible]	[illegible]	[illegible]	[illegible]	[illegible]	[illegible]	[illegible]	[illegible]	[illegible]	[illegible]	[illegible]	[illegible]	[illegible]	[illegible]	[illegible]	[illegible]	[illegible]	[illegible]
	Japan	[illegible]	[illegible]	[illegible]	[illegible]	[illegible]	[illegible]	[illegible]	[illegible]	[illegible]	[illegible]	[illegible]	[illegible]	[illegible]	[illegible]	[illegible]	[illegible]	[illegible]	[illegible]
	USA	[illegible]	[illegible]	[illegible]	[illegible]	[illegible]	[illegible]	[illegible]	[illegible]	[illegible]	[illegible]	[illegible]	[illegible]	[illegible]	[illegible]	[illegible]	[illegible]	[illegible]	[illegible]
Brunei Darussalam	India	[illegible]	[illegible]	[illegible]	[illegible]	[illegible]	[illegible]	[illegible]	[illegible]	[illegible]	[illegible]	[illegible]	[illegible]	[illegible]	[illegible]	[illegible]	[illegible]	[illegible]	[illegible]
	China	[illegible]	[illegible]	[illegible]	[illegible]	[illegible]	[illegible]	[illegible]	[illegible]	[illegible]	[illegible]	[illegible]	[illegible]	[illegible]	[illegible]	[illegible]	[illegible]	[illegible]	[illegible]
	Japan	[illegible]	[illegible]	[illegible]	[illegible]	[illegible]	[illegible]	[illegible]	[illegible]	[illegible]	[illegible]	[illegible]	[illegible]	[illegible]	[illegible]	[illegible]	[illegible]	[illegible]	[illegible]
	USA	[illegible]	[illegible]	[illegible]	[illegible]	[illegible]	[illegible]	[illegible]	[illegible]	[illegible]	[illegible]	[illegible]	[illegible]	[illegible]	[illegible]	[illegible]	[illegible]	[illegible]	[illegible]
Cambodia	India	[illegible]	[illegible]	[illegible]	[illegible]	[illegible]	[illegible]	[illegible]	[illegible]	[illegible]	[illegible]	[illegible]	[illegible]	[illegible]	[illegible]	[illegible]	[illegible]	[illegible]	[illegible]
	China	[illegible]	[illegible]	[illegible]	[illegible]	[illegible]	[illegible]	[illegible]	[illegible]	[illegible]	[illegible]	[illegible]	[illegible]	[illegible]	[illegible]	[illegible]	[illegible]	[illegible]	[illegible]
	Japan	[illegible]	[illegible]	[illegible]	[illegible]	[illegible]	[illegible]	[illegible]	[illegible]	[illegible]	[illegible]	[illegible]	[illegible]	[illegible]	[illegible]	[illegible]	[illegible]	[illegible]	[illegible]
	USA	[illegible]	[illegible]	[illegible]	[illegible]	[illegible]	[illegible]	[illegible]	[illegible]	[illegible]	[illegible]	[illegible]	[illegible]	[illegible]	[illegible]	[illegible]	[illegible]	[illegible]	[illegible]
Indonesia	India	[illegible]	[illegible]	[illegible]	[illegible]	[illegible]	[illegible]	[illegible]	[illegible]	[illegible]	[illegible]	[illegible]	[illegible]	[illegible]	[illegible]	[illegible]	[illegible]	[illegible]	[illegible]
	China			[illegible]	[illegible]	[illegible]	[illegible]	[illegible]	[illegible]	[illegible]	[illegible]	[illegible]	[illegible]	[illegible]	[illegible]	[illegible]	[illegible]	[illegible]	[illegible]
	Japan	[illegible]	[illegible]	[illegible]	[illegible]	[illegible]	[illegible]	[illegible]	[illegible]	[illegible]	[illegible]	[illegible]	[illegible]	[illegible]	[illegible]	[illegible]	[illegible]	[illegible]	[illegible]
	USA	[illegible]	[illegible]	[illegible]	[illegible]	[illegible]	[illegible]	[illegible]	[illegible]	[illegible]	[illegible]	[illegible]	[illegible]	[illegible]	[illegible]	[illegible]	[illegible]	[illegible]	[illegible]
Lao PDR	India	[illegible]	[illegible]	[illegible]	[illegible]	[illegible]	[illegible]	[illegible]	[illegible]	[illegible]	[illegible]	[illegible]	[illegible]	[illegible]	[illegible]	[illegible]	[illegible]	[illegible]	[illegible]
	China	[illegible]	[illegible]	[illegible]	[illegible]	[illegible]	[illegible]	[illegible]	[illegible]	[illegible]	[illegible]	[illegible]	[illegible]	[illegible]	[illegible]	[illegible]	[illegible]	[illegible]	[illegible]
	Japan	[illegible]	[illegible]	[illegible]	[illegible]	[illegible]	[illegible]	[illegible]	[illegible]	[illegible]	[illegible]	[illegible]	[illegible]	[illegible]	[illegible]	[illegible]	[illegible]	[illegible]	[illegible]
	USA	[illegible]	[illegible]	[illegible]	[illegible]	[illegible]	[illegible]	[illegible]	[illegible]	[illegible]	[illegible]	[illegible]	[illegible]	[illegible]	[illegible]	[illegible]	[illegible]	[illegible]	[illegible]
Malaysia	India	[illegible]	[illegible]	[illegible]	[illegible]	[illegible]	[illegible]	[illegible]	[illegible]	[illegible]	[illegible]	[illegible]	[illegible]	[illegible]	[illegible]	[illegible]	[illegible]	[illegible]	[illegible]
	China	[illegible]	[illegible]	[illegible]	[illegible]	[illegible]	[illegible]	[illegible]	[illegible]	[illegible]	[illegible]	[illegible]	[illegible]	[illegible]	[illegible]	[illegible]	[illegible]	[illegible]	[illegible]
	Japan	[illegible]	[illegible]	[illegible]	[illegible]	[illegible]	[illegible]	[illegible]	[illegible]	[illegible]	[illegible]	[illegible]	[illegible]	[illegible]	[illegible]	[illegible]	[illegible]	[illegible]	[illegible]
	USA	[illegible]	[illegible]	[illegible]	[illegible]	[illegible]	[illegible]	[illegible]	[illegible]	[illegible]	[illegible]	[illegible]	[illegible]	[illegible]	[illegible]	[illegible]	[illegible]	[illegible]	[illegible]
Myanmar	India	[illegible]	[illegible]	[illegible]	[illegible]	[illegible]	[illegible]	[illegible]	[illegible]	[illegible]	[illegible]	[illegible]	[illegible]	[illegible]	[illegible]	[illegible]	[illegible]	[illegible]	[illegible]
	China	[illegible]	[illegible]	[illegible]	[illegible]	[illegible]	[illegible]	[illegible]	[illegible]	[illegible]	[illegible]	[illegible]	[illegible]	[illegible]	[illegible]	[illegible]	[illegible]	[illegible]	[illegible]
	Japan	[illegible]	[illegible]	[illegible]	[illegible]	[illegible]	[illegible]	[illegible]	[illegible]	[illegible]	[illegible]	[illegible]	[illegible]	[illegible]	[illegible]	[illegible]	[illegible]	[illegible]	[illegible]
	USA	[illegible]	[illegible]	[illegible]	[illegible]	[illegible]	[illegible]	[illegible]	[illegible]	[illegible]	[illegible]	[illegible]	[illegible]	[illegible]	[illegible]	[illegible]	[illegible]	[illegible]	[illegible]
Philippines	India	[illegible]	[illegible]	[illegible]	[illegible]	[illegible]	[illegible]	[illegible]	[illegible]	[illegible]	[illegible]	[illegible]	[illegible]	[illegible]	[illegible]	[illegible]	[illegible]	[illegible]	[illegible]
	China	[illegible]	[illegible]	[illegible]	[illegible]	[illegible]	[illegible]	[illegible]	[illegible]	[illegible]	[illegible]	[illegible]	[illegible]	[illegible]	[illegible]	[illegible]	[illegible]	[illegible]	[illegible]
	Japan	[illegible]	[illegible]	[illegible]	[illegible]	[illegible]	[illegible]	[illegible]	[illegible]	[illegible]	[illegible]	[illegible]	[illegible]	[illegible]	[illegible]	[illegible]	[illegible]	[illegible]	[illegible]
	USA	[illegible]	[illegible]	[illegible]	[illegible]	[illegible]	[illegible]	[illegible]	[illegible]	[illegible]	[illegible]	[illegible]	[illegible]	[illegible]	[illegible]	[illegible]	[illegible]	[illegible]	[illegible]
Singapore	India	[illegible]	[illegible]	[illegible]	[illegible]	[illegible]	[illegible]	[illegible]	[illegible]	[illegible]	[illegible]	[illegible]	[illegible]	[illegible]	[illegible]	[illegible]	[illegible]	[illegible]	[illegible]
	China	[illegible]	[illegible]	[illegible]	[illegible]	[illegible]	[illegible]	[illegible]	[illegible]	[illegible]	[illegible]	[illegible]	[illegible]	[illegible]	[illegible]	[illegible]	[illegible]	[illegible]	[illegible]
	Japan	[illegible]	[illegible]	[illegible]	[illegible]	[illegible]	[illegible]	[illegible]	[illegible]	[illegible]	[illegible]	[illegible]	[illegible]	[illegible]	[illegible]	[illegible]	[illegible]	[illegible]	[illegible]
	USA	[illegible]	[illegible]	[illegible]	[illegible]	[illegible]	[illegible]	[illegible]	[illegible]	[illegible]	[illegible]	[illegible]	[illegible]	[illegible]	[illegible]	[illegible]	[illegible]	[illegible]	[illegible]
Thailand	India	[illegible]	[illegible]	[illegible]	[illegible]	[illegible]	[illegible]	[illegible]	[illegible]	[illegible]	[illegible]	[illegible]	[illegible]	[illegible]	[illegible]	[illegible]	[illegible]	[illegible]	[illegible]
	China	[illegible]	[illegible]	[illegible]	[illegible]	[illegible]	[illegible]	[illegible]	[illegible]	[illegible]	[illegible]	[illegible]	[illegible]	[illegible]	[illegible]	[illegible]	[illegible]	[illegible]	[illegible]
	Japan	[illegible]	[illegible]	[illegible]	[illegible]	[illegible]	[illegible]	[illegible]	[illegible]	[illegible]	[illegible]	[illegible]	[illegible]	[illegible]	[illegible]	[illegible]	[illegible]	[illegible]	[illegible]
	USA	[illegible]	[illegible]	[illegible]	[illegible]	[illegible]	[illegible]	[illegible]	[illegible]	[illegible]	[illegible]	[illegible]	[illegible]	[illegible]	[illegible]	[illegible]	[illegible]	[illegible]	[illegible]
Viet Nam	India	[illegible]	[illegible]	[illegible]	[illegible]	[illegible]	[illegible]	[illegible]	[illegible]	[illegible]	[illegible]	[illegible]	[illegible]	[illegible]	[illegible]	[illegible]	[illegible]	[illegible]	[illegible]
	China	[illegible]	[illegible]	[illegible]	[illegible]	[illegible]	[illegible]	[illegible]	[illegible]	[illegible]	[illegible]	[illegible]	[illegible]	[illegible]	[illegible]	[illegible]	[illegible]	[illegible]	[illegible]
	Japan	[illegible]	[illegible]	[illegible]	[illegible]	[illegible]	[illegible]	[illegible]	[illegible]	[illegible]	[illegible]	[illegible]	[illegible]	[illegible]	[illegible]	[illegible]	[illegible]	[illegible]	[illegible]
	USA	[illegible]	[illegible]	[illegible]	[illegible]	[illegible]	[illegible]	[illegible]	[illegible]	[illegible]	[illegible]	[illegible]	[illegible]	[illegible]	[illegible]	[illegible]	[illegible]	[illegible]	[illegible]

ASEAN Nations Exports to India as a Percentage of Total World Exports

		2009	2010	2011	2012	2013	2014	2015	2016	2017
	India	3.28	4.21	3.70	3.47	3.56	3.38	3.46	3.28	3.45
ASEAN	China	10.05	11.12	11.28	11.33	12.47	11.90	12.40	12.51	14.19
	Japan	9.63	10.23	10.31	10.17	10.79	9.25	8.70	8.38	7.99
	USA	10.12	10.41	8.46	8.57	9.25	9.37	10.71	11.37	10.72
	India	0.86	6.18	8.09	8.76	8.15	9.13	9.10	9.58	4.75
Brunei Darussalam	China	4.07	7.22	4.14	2.67	1.12	0.20	1.49	5.16	10.71
	Japan	46.49	43.21	43.42	43.44	40.21	37.15	36.34	34.06	20.42
	USA	0.60	0.00	0.10	0.73	0.00	0.19	0.83	0.21	0.47
Cambodia	India	0.10	0.00	0.24	0.16	0.00	0.12	0.12	0.22	0.29
	China	0.33	2.13	2.99	3.34	4.21	5.28	5.05	6.05	4.77
	Japan	1.60	2.12	2.09	3.46	5.60	5.11	6.74	0.21	0.01
	USA	31.15	50.13	41.15	29.17	30.12	29.64	25.19	21.31	21.09
Indonesia	India	6.38	6.37	6.55	6.58	7.12	6.96	7.79	6.96	[illegible]
	China	9.87	10.09	16.27	11.40	12.32	10.01	10.01	11.57	10.40
	Japan	15.94	16.23	16.57	15.06	15.15	13.14	11.90	11.09	10.64
	USA	9.35	9.32	8.09	7.83	9.12	9.39	10.81	11.12	10.34

Lao PDR	India	0.00	0.00	0.01	0.00	0.00	0.12	1.11	2.87	1.18
	China	0.23	12.07	5.55	6.75	12.12	27.42	34.82	42.42	34.19
	Japan	0.75	11.21	2.56	1.91	2.32	2.08	1.66	1.69	1.96
	USA	1.70	2.03	1.84	0.44	1.64	0.97	0.79	0.54	0.62
Malaysia	India	3.07	13.64	4.03	4.17	4.26	4.17	2.21	4.07	3.69
	China	12.15	30.32	13.12	12.64	13.12	12.04	18.82	12.51	13.50
	Japan	9.84	10.37	11.64	11.87	11.23	10.79	7.83	8.09	7.99
	USA	10.95	10.03	8.26	8.65	8.32	8.41	8.06	10.21	9.48
Myanmar	India	15.17	3.37	13.17	12.50	9.23	7.58	2.81	8.77	4.71
	China	7.40	12.01	3.74	21.32	27.23	36.50	30.01	41.66	42.50
	Japan	2.63	3.23	4.16	4.31	4.24	4.74	9.09	5.60	5.85
	USA	0.00	0.00	0.21	0.20	0.00	0.39	0.61	1.27	1.73
Philippines	India	0.52	11.64	0.81	0.63	1.63	0.48	1.88	0.56	0.80
	China	7.64	1.45	12.70	11.85	12.24	13.64	13.07	11.00	11.06
	Japan	16.16	15.12	18.46	19.00	21.24	22.39	6.73	20.73	16.10

Lao PDR	India	0.00	0.00	0.01	0.00	0.00	0.12	1.11	2.87	4.48
	China	0.23	12.07	5.55	6.75	12.12	27.42	34.82	42.42	34.19
	Japan	0.75	11.21	2.56	1.91	2.32	2.08	1.66	1.69	1.96
	USA	1.70	2.03	1.84	0.44	1.64	0.97	0.79	0.54	0.62
Malaysia	India	3.07	13.64	4.03	4.17	4.26	4.17	2.21	4.07	3.60
	China	12.15	30.32	13.12	12.64	13.12	12.04	18.82	12.51	13.50
	Japan	9.84	10.37	11.64	11.87	11.23	10.79	7.83	8.09	7.99
	USA	10.95	10.03	8.26	8.65	8.32	8.41	8.06	10.21	9.48
Myanmar	India	15.17	3.37	13.17	12.50	9.23	7.58	2.81	8.77	4.71
	China	7.49	12.01	3.74	21.32	27.23	36.50	38.01	41.66	42.59
	Japan	2.63	3.23	4.16	4.31	4.24	4.74	5.09	5.60	5.85
	USA	0.00	0.00	0.21	0.20	0.00	0.39	0.61	1.27	1.73
Philippines	India	0.52	11.64	0.81	0.63	1.63	0.48	1.88	0.56	0.80
	China	7.64	1.45	12.70	11.85	12.24	13.64	13.67	11.00	11.06
	Japan	16.16	15.12	18.46	19.00	21.24	22.39	6.23	20.73	16.10
	USA	17.60	15.63	14.76	14.22	14.23	13.95	10.83	15.39	14.52

Singapore	India	3.46	4.24	3.44	2.84	3.23	2.77	1.88	2.97	2.87
	China	9.71	10.64	10.25	10.66	12.23	13.16	13.67	13.11	14.09
	Japan	4.53	5.74	4.41	4.35	4.22	4.03	6.23	4.31	4.46
	USA	6.49	6.15	5.25	5.23	5.23	5.22	10.83	6.40	6.13
Thailand	India	2.11	2.04	2.33	2.39	2.23	2.47	1.37	2.39	2.74
	China	10.57	11.12	11.79	11.72	12.23	11.02	20.26	11.06	12.44
	Japan	10.32	11.79	10.72	10.73	10.12	9.59	15.41	9.55	9.45
	USA	10.94	10.26	9.79	9.93	10.23	10.50	6.84	11.38	11.21
Viet Nam	India	0.00	1.15	1.60	1.55	2.63	1.66	1.60	1.52	1.76
	China	8.62	10.18	11.48	10.78	10.64	10.03	29.90	12.42	16.59
	Japan	11.10	11.00	11.13	11.39	10.12	9.79	8.66	8.31	7.88
	USA	20.06	20.64	17.41	17.12	18.12	19.36	4.70	21.70	19.46

Sources: Author's Calculations based unctad.com

0.29% of its exports are directed towards India during the year 2017.

The overall analysis presents that the exports of "Brunei Darussalam, Cambodia, Indonesia, Laos PDR, Malaysia, Philippines, Thailand and Vietnam to India", as a percentage of their respective exports initially decreased during Pre-AIFTA period from 2000 to 2009 and then increased during the period from 2009 to 2017. The reversal of the decrease in exports of ASEAN to India could be due to "ASEAN-India Free Trade Agreement" (AIFTA) that came into effect in January 2010. There was a gradual rise in the respective exports of these economies to India over these 9 years owing to the gradual reduction of tariff levels between India and ASEAN. A comparative analysis of exports to China, Japan and USA observes that USA's share in ASEAN total exports decreased from 2000 to 2017 for almost all the countries of ASEAN except for Cambodia, Indonesia and Thailand, this is the result of growing integration in the Asian continent. One significant observation is that declining and flattening export share of Japan with the ASEAN member states (except for Philippines and Cambodia) and increase in China's share over the study period 2000 to 2017 concerning the export share. Japan has been the traditional partner with the ASEAN countries and has been a vital founder-member of the "Asia Pacific Economic Co-operation (APEC)" group. However, the growing integration of ASEAN with China, with the China-ASEAN FTA being signed in the year 2002 which resulted in the elimination of first six signatories tariff levels up to 90% and increase in the total trade volumes.

4.4.2 ASEAN Nations Imports from India as a Percentage of Total World Imports

The ASEAN group was one of the biggest importers in the world. The total imports by ASEAN stood by

USD 1.17 trillion during the year 2017. The share of ASEAN's imports from India as percentage of world imports has been increasing from 2.82 in 2000 to 3.64 in 2008, and fallen to 1.73 in 2009, could be due to sub-prime crisis, and thereafter gradually risen to 2.27 in 2017 as a result of gradual reduction of the tariff lines on account of India-ASEAN FTA. Similarly the share of China also found an increase in total share of ASEAN imports, with the reduction in the tariff levels from 5.8% in 2000 and 13.78% in 2009 and this gradually increased to 2017 % for the year 2017, China – the new rising economy of the Asia using massive mass-production techniques in its industries and conquering the market with its cheap exports has an excellent demand for imports which is being catered by the ASEAN group. There was a decline in the import shares of Japan and USA from the ASEAN which could be observed from the Table. 4.3 on the ASEAN Nations Imports to India as a Percentage of Total World Imports. India's import share with the ASEAN countries has an upward trend observed for 7 countries of ASEAN, especially after AIFTA from 2009 onwards, and declining trend could be observed with Singapore, Malaysia and the Philippines. With India and Philippines FTA tariff reduction framework coming into effect from Normal track 1 from 2018 and Normal Track 2 from 2016 and sensitive tract from 2019 the share would be on the rise in future. The same is in the case of Thailand and Singapore, where the tariff reduction framework which has been active since 2016. Like the share of exports, ASEAN imports from China also found to be drastically raising during the study period which is evident from the growing integration of ASEAN and Chinese economies, which has been affecting the countries like USA & Japan. The share of Japan has been declining significantly (except Cambodia with 2.53% in the year 2000 to 4.70 in 2017) from 2000- 2017 and the share of USA also found to be declining significantly during the period of the study.

Table 4.3 ASEAN Nations Imports to India as a Percentage of Total World Imports

		2000	2001	2002	2003	2004	2005	2006	2007	2008	2009	2010	2011	2012	2013	2014	2015	2016	2017
ASEAN	India	[illegible]	[illegible]	[illegible]	4.77	3.39	3.76	[illegible]	3.38	3.64	[illegible]	2.91	2.31	[illegible]	2.01	1.99	[illegible]	3.28	[illegible]
	China	1.80	7.17	8.09	6.78	10.69	12.06	[illegible]	[illegible]	[illegible]	[illegible]	[illegible]	[illegible]	11.84	14.82	17.10	10.83	13.11	[illegible]
	Japan	13.87	13.46	12.17	13.14	13.33	12.84	11.71	11.48	12.33	13.46	12.36	11.01	11.16	9.74	8.78	9.16	8.38	9.10
	USA	8.43	8.66	3.71	8.68	7.92	7.33	7.84	7.12	7.58	9.87	9.10	8.41	7.82	7.95	7.87	7.79	11.37	7.88
Brunei Darussalam	India	9.49	9.04	9.82	9.16	5.97	7.30	7.38	4.58	3.63	3.83	1.28	0.90	0.84	1.23	1.10	1.14	[illegible]	1.64
	China	5.11	9.76	7.49	8.29	9.59	10.28	11.29	9.48	9.65	3.20	7.13	7.46	8.01	11.63	9.95	11.64	5.18	20.92
	Japan	45.68	44.76	39.01	39.47	38.63	38.45	50.12	51.49	42.89	9.33	10.37	7.00	8.06	6.02	4.05	7.80	54.68	3.92
	USA	9.32	9.55	10.47	6.45	6.78	7.33	5.91	8.85	9.38	13.20	10.01	12.10	9.72	7.23	9.05	10.54	1.51	9.45
Cambodia	India	1.30	2.10	1.96	2.68	1.31	3.27	1.79	1.98	3.73	22.35	1.23	1.23	1.48	1.78	1.55	0.98	0.23	0.82
	China	8.28	8.96	11.20	11.08	14.82	18.28	14.30	[illegible]	18.56	[illegible]	24.30	28.45	29.84	[illegible]	[illegible]	[illegible]	[illegible]	37.72
	Japan	[illegible]	[illegible]	[illegible]	[illegible]	[illegible]	[illegible]	[illegible]	[illegible]	[illegible]	[illegible]	[illegible]	[illegible]	[illegible]	[illegible]	[illegible]	[illegible]	[illegible]	[illegible]
	USA	1.81	1.34	1.15	1.89	1.61	3.68	1.31	1.98	3.86	2.93	2.12	7.91	2.37	2.47	2.25	1.85	21.31	1.37
Indonesia	India			[illegible]	3.18	3.31	4.78	3.82	3.98	4.84	2.28	2.12	2.44	2.85	2.78	2.22	1.91	4.94	2.38
	China		6.76	6.08	5.28	6.17	8.29	7.09	11.00		14.44	12.13	14.77	15.83	14.01	17.19	20.41	11.57	22.78
	Japan				21.22	22.36	20.75	20.99	20.03	18.87	10.87	12.69	10.92	11.83	10.01	9.33	9.30	11.09	9.72
	USA	7.44	6.39	3.87	3.48	3.65	3.05	4.28	3.98	4.84	7.33	6.94	6.69	6.04	4.26	4.48	5.32	11.12	5.17
Lao PDR	India	0.70	0.41	0.48	0.48	1.94	0.53	0.83	1.44		0.21	0.31	0.14	0.35	1.05	0.44	0.58	0.87	0.49
	China	5.04	8.64	8.12	13.48	10.55	9.34	11.38	9.87	10.64	3.59	10.33	26.73	19.84	15.01	12.93	18.88	42.42	20.37
	Japan	3.34	2.16	2.00	2.04	1.66	3.41	1.21	1.15	3.44	3.86	2.38	1.64	2.95	3.85	2.63	3.41	1.49	2.36
	USA	0.61	0.47	0.68	0.68	0.62	0.82	0.48	0.68	0.71	0.20	0.12	0.56	0.40	1.47	0.49	0.52	0.48	0.46
Malaysia	India	1.34	1.81	2.80	3.70	2.13	2.17	2.20	2.82	3.52	13.92	2.18	1.78	1.92	3.39	1.92	2.21	4.07	3.21
	China	3.98	4.16	7.81	8.76	9.83	18.83	13.18	21.88	12.83	3.83	31.48	31.19	16.84	14.84	14.91	18.83	12.81	[illegible]
	Japan	13.07	13.91	11.13	10.72	10.08	9.43	8.88	9.21	10.62	12.48	11.21	11.94	10.28	9.05	8.01	7.83	8.09	7.59
	USA	[illegible]	[illegible]	[illegible]	12.45	14.21	12.98	12.60	[illegible]	[illegible]	[illegible]	[illegible]	[illegible]	[illegible]	[illegible]	[illegible]	[illegible]	[illegible]	[illegible]

Myanmar	India	2.83	3.13	4.91	7.19	7.67	8.58	12.25	8.62	8.73	1.83	4.51	3.37	3.86	3.82	4.65	2.81	6.77	3.67
	China	4.76	6.56	6.77	9.57	12.28	9.07	4.17	4.67	5.97	23.95	24.65	22.47	25.80	30.51	30.95	38.01	41.66	31.77
	Japan	8.28	5.58	4.18	3.05	6.78	6.17	6.09	8.02	3.98	22.48	3.23	4.90	11.97	10.82	10.16	9.09	3.60	3.48
	USA	2.83	3.13	4.45	6.23	9.20	8.58	12.76	8.62	9.46	21.18	3.33	2.48	1.96	1.23	2.98	0.81	1.27	3.86
Philippines	India	1.00	1.22	1.25	1.18	1.15	1.15	1.38	1.24	1.26	1.18	1.33	1.10	1.16	1.28	1.41	1.82	6.56	1.44
	China	2.36	3.09	3.79	4.58	6.11	6.83	7.16	7.90	7.55	8.86	8.31	10.31	10.91	13.02	15.38	16.35	11.00	18.17
	Japan	14.73	15.13	12.04	15.92	20.12	17.47	16.70	14.47	13.76	12.13	13.14	11.01	10.86	9.01	8.10	9.60	20.75	11.34
	USA	19.42	19.63	28.44	21.88	18.54	18.87	16.08	18.09	12.81	21.86	11.88	10.68	11.41	11.65	8.95	10.88	15.38	7.91
Singapore	India	3.76	3.16	5.83	7.81	5.84	4.06	4.77	4.46	3.74	3.58	3.57	3.85	3.44	3.81	3.10	3.83	3.47	3.58
	China	4.82	3.89	9.82	7.76	9.79	10.09	11.86	12.62	11.27	19.78	11.23	19.27	19.27	11.82	11.72	13.97	13.11	14.29
	Japan	4.84	4.84	4.53	3.34	3.00	8.01	1.00	4.87	4.42	7.44	8.21	7.38	4.21	3.23	4.30	4.30	3.31	4.11
	USA	14.78	16.73	14.56	13.77	15.64	13.98	13.64	12.18	11.98	21.58	17.34	10.58	9.69	10.85	10.08	10.85	4.40	10.64
Thailand	India	2.03	2.62	5.22	3.48	1.83	0.91	2.34	2.28	1.93	1.29	1.89	1.32	1.29	1.98	3.02	1.90	2.38	1.73
	China	5.44	6.00	7.63	8.00	8.67	9.44	10.37	12.13	11.18	22.73	3.83	23.33	24.92	13.43	12.05	20.34	11.09	19.84
	Japan	14.65	15.74	14.60	14.78	15.98	15.53	12.79	12.78	11.18	28.73	21.96	18.48	20.01	16.73	14.00	15.11	9.95	14.51
	USA	11.78	11.39	9.60	9.47	7.70	7.58	6.74	6.87	6.41	6.53	6.89	5.85	5.21	6.14	6.29	6.84	11.38	4.67
Viet Nam	India	3.81	3.43	0.67	1.29	5.11	4.79	5.22	3.65	3.53	0.83	2.36	2.30	0.19	2.45	3.02	1.60	1.52	1.74
	China	9.67	10.40	12.90	15.98	17.35	18.19	18.56	26.17	35.48	23.83	34.81	23.84	24.34	24.81	24.96	29.60	13.43	26.19
	Japan	17.78	16.70	18.39	14.48	13.37	15.81	13.18	12.94	13.51	20.75	13.81	9.74	10.12	9.11	8.78	8.64	8.31	2.43
	USA	1.32	2.63	2.83	3.79	4.30	2.71	2.08	3.78	4.23	4.27	4.03	4.24	4.14	4.87	3.00	4.70	21.78	4.12

Sources: Author`s Calculations based unctad.com

4.4.3 India's Trade (Exports and Imports) as a percentage of ASEAN Trade

Over time, the overall trade trajectory between India and the ASEAN countries witnessed a change in importance for each other's market. When compared to the bountiful trade volume that ASEAN countries have in the world market, the trade volume (export and import volume) of India remained less. India's presence in the ASEAN's top 10 import partner countries is inconsiderable, but ASEAN imported around 11.10 billion valued imports from India, accounting for a share of 2.27% of overall Imports of from the world during the year 2017. Similarly, India's export share of top ten products at HS-02 stood at US$ 165.46 billion, which is about 62% of the gross exports during 2017. The value of exports of India to ASEAN was 12.78 billion US dollars, which is 7.75% of its total exports.

Chart 4.1India's Exports to ASEAN Countries as Percentage of its Total Exports

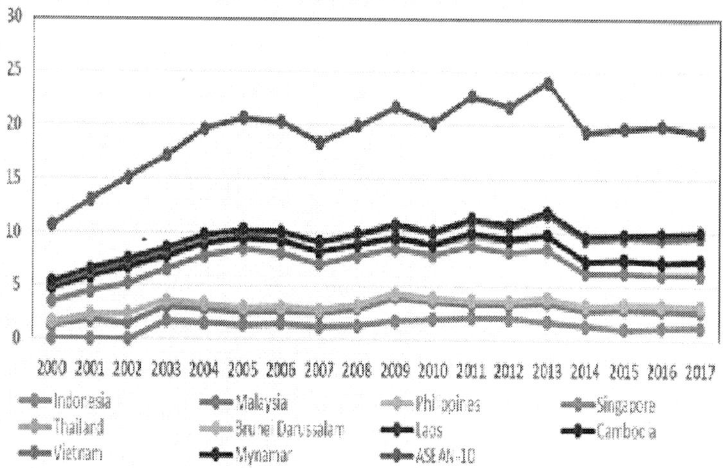

Source: Author's calculation based on data from www.unctad.org

The above Chart. 4.1 presents the exports of India to ASEAN countries out of its total exports in percentage terms from the year 2000 till the year 2017. Exports of India to ASEAN has been remarkably on the rise from 2000 till 2006, followed by a decline during the period 2007 and 2008 could be owing to the slowdown of the global economy. The percentage share of exports has been revived after the year 2009 (10.85 %), and this rose to 12.03% during the year 2013 when the FTA agreement has come into effect between India and the ASEAN nations since the year 2010. The year 2014 experienced the slowdown in the world economies owing to European Union crisis this also had effected the over the trade of both the sides along with the implementation of "Goods and Services Taxation"(GST) in India since February 2015 and demonetization initiative of 2016 has effected the export regime of the country. Among the ASEAN 10 countries Singapore has the highest trade share with India, the export share for the year 2000 is 1.857% and this has gradually increased to 2.880 percent for the year 2017, though the export share received a short decline before and after crisis period (4.256% in the year 2007 and 4.005% in the year 2010), the next largest export partner among the ASEAN has been Malaysia where India always holds an export share of more than 1 % during the period of study. This place has been gradually occupied by Vietnam where India's export percentage share is on rising with 0.461 per cent during the year 2000, and this gradually rose to 2.246 per cent in the year 2017, the rise has been much after the FTA between India and ASEAN with the special CLMV (Cambodia, Lao PDR, Myanmar, Vietnam) initiative implemented by India to accelerate the investment and trade with the ASEAN. Indonesia has always been an important with the total volume of India's trade doubled since 2007 with US$7 billion to 31.31 billion during the year 2017 and India has always maintained a consistent trade share with Thailand of above 1. The percentage of exports to the Philippines is 0.411 per cent during the year 2000, and this reached 0.535 per cent during the year 2017. Myanmar is one country whose trade share has been on the rise with India for the study period, and its share of trade which was 0.102 per cent in the year 2000 rose to 0.426 per cent in the year 2017 due to FTA between India and ASEAN and owing to the CLMV initiative in the most recent years. The export share of India with Brunei Lao PDR and Cambodia has been minimal, owing to the smaller sizes of their economies.

The trends in the exports of India to the ASEAN nations are further analyzed here. Table. 4.4 presents the value of exponential growth, correlation, values of Coefficient of variation along with the 't' test ratios for the exports of India to the ASEAN countries from 2000 to 2017. The Exponential growth rate is measured for the overall study period to observe the growth trends of exports of India to the ASEAN economies. The Exponential growth values could be observed to be positive of Malaysia (1.041), Singapore (1.840), Brunei Darussalam (6.910), Lao PDR (9.437), Cambodia (4.240) and Vietnam (9.827) where India's export share has been on rise, especially with respect to Vietnam where the export share rose from 0.461 per cent to 2.246 per cent during the year 2017 the exponential growth has been high in the case of Cambodia and Brunei but negative in the case of Indonesia where the export percentage share of India actually declined since the year 2003 which was 1.763 per cent to 1.235 during the year 2017. Philippines which declined from 0.411 during the year 2000 to 0.535 in the year 2017 and Thailand where gradual decline and revival in the year 2017.

The correlation coefficient presents an insignificant relationship over the years for most of the countries, except in the case of Vietnam (0.979) and Myanmar (0.867), where there is export consistency throughout the study. The CV value has been highest in the case of Vietnam, with a 95 % significance level followed by Myanmar and Cambodia. The 't' values have been insignificant, with the highest value exhibited in the case of Vietnam (9.382).

Table. 4.4 India's Exports to ASEAN countries as a percentage of its Total Exports

Country	Total Period Exponential Growth (2000-2017)	Correlation Value 'r'	Coefficient of Variation (CV)%	't' ratio
Indonesia	-1.038	-0.202	0.041	0.171
Malaysia	1.041*	0.386	0.042	0.352
Philippines	-1.565	-0.316	0.1	0.433
Singapore	1.840*	0.29	0.084	0.362
Thailand	-1.024	-0.419	0.178	0.795
Brunei Darussalam	6.910*	0.364	0.133	0.588
Lao PDR	5.417*	0.474	0.224	1.05
Cambodia	4.340*	0.308	0.561	2.921
Vietnam	5.827*	0.529	0.958	9.382
Myanmar	6.422*	0.867	0.589	3.785
ASEAN-10	3.910*	0.718	0.512	3.023

Source: Author's calculation based on Appendix Table

*indicate significant at 1% level

**indicate significant at 5% level,

***indicate significant at 10% level

CV indicates co-efficient of variation during the period 2000 to 2017

The Chart. 4.2 explains imports of India from the ASEAN countries as a percentage of total imports of India. Over the time, ASEAN imports have been on rising till the year 2007 which is 10.023 per cent, thereafter there was a decline in the percentage of imports from India during the crisis period of 2008, after which there was a revival, the ASEAN total share is 10.21 per cent during the year 2017 in total imports of India. The "Look

Chart 4.2 India's Imports from the ASEAN Countries as Percentage of its Total Imports

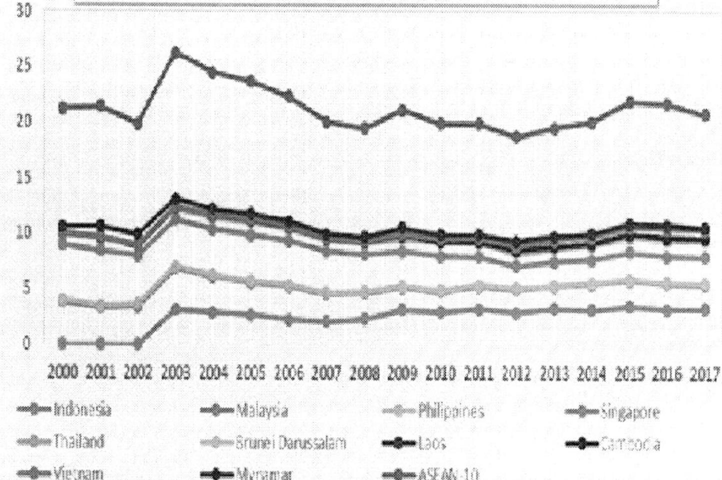

Source: Author's calculation based on data extracted from www.unctad.org

East Policy" initiative and the up-gradation of the policy to "Act East Policy" has revived share of India's trade with the ASEAN. Singapore became fifth largest import source for India during 2018, an important finding is that India's share of imports from Singapore has been declining gradually as the country was the third-largest source of imports during the year 2016, this could also be observed in the declining import shares of the country from 5.017 per cent in 2000 to 2.428 per cent during 2017. Indonesia has been one of the prominent trading partners and import value, which is 3.10 per cent in 2003 and 3.212 per cent during the year 2017. The import share of Malaysia in the total value of imports has also been gradually reduced to 2.22 per cent in 2017 from 3.84 per cent in 2000, Malaysia emerged as the 13th largest trade source for imports for the country with 6.5 billion import value. Thailand import share has been more than once throughout the study period which is 1.018 per cent during the year 2000 and this accelerated to 1.479 during the year 2017, the country has been emerging as a significant trade partner to India. Vietnam's trade share has been on the rise from the year 2000 from 0.071 per cent to 0.789 per cent in the year 2017, Vietnam proceeded to become 12th largest trading partner for imports to India with 6.7 billion trade during the year 2017. Myanmar's import share has been on decline, the import share from the Philippines, Brunei, Los and Cambodia has been insignificant owing to their smaller size of the economies however India's CLMV approach there has been quite good progress, over the years China has occupied larger chunk of the country's imports from Asia replacing number of the Asian partners.

The imports share of India is further analyzed in the Table. 4.5 presenting exponential growth rate, correlation, coefficient of variation and the 't' ratio. The exponential growth rate captures that the imports growth from Indonesia, Thailand, Brunei Darussalam, Laos, Cambodia, Vietnam has been showing significant growth values with Laos showing the highest 50.411 per cent growth during 2000 to 2017, which was 0.00 per cent during the initial study period to 0.021 per cent during the year 2017. Malaysia, Philippines, Singapore, Myanmar registering a negative growth as could be (Chart. 4.2, Table 4.5) seen. Similarly. Significant correlation values could be found in the case of Lao PDR with 0.858 and Vietnam 0.933. The Coefficient of Variation is found to be highest for Singapore with 91 per cent, Vietnam with 87 per cent variation followed by Lao PDR 73.5 per cent and Malaysia 73.1 per cent and Myanmar 68.7 per cent, the overall coefficient of variation for the ASEAN rests at 20 per cent. The t ratios present highly insignificant relations between the period with Singapore the t ratio at 12.756, Vietnam as high as 9.932 and lease being 1.363 of Indonesia.

Table. 4.5 India's Imports from the ASEAN Countries as Percentage of its Total Imports

Country	Total Period Exponential Growth (2000-2017)	Correlation Value 'r'	Coefficient of Variation ◇ (CV) %	't' ratio
Indonesia	1.964*	0.529	0.28	1.363
Malaysia	-3.804	-0.855	0.731	5.819
Philippines	-4.601	-0.742	0.551	3.388
Singapore	-5.9	-0.955	0.913	12.756
Thailand	2.276*	0.777	0.803	3.951
Brunei Darussalam	23.065*	0.634	0.403	2.139
Laos	50.411*	0.858	0.735	5.893
Cambodia	14.781*	0.672	0.452	2.517
Vietnam	17.547*	0.933	0.87	9.932
Myanmar	-6.833	-0.829	0.687	5.058
ANSEAN-10	-0.692	-0.455	0.207	0.96

Source: Author's calculation based on Appendix Table.

*Indicate significant at 1% level,

**Indicate significant at 5% level

***Indicate significant at 10% level

◇C.V. indicates co-efficient of variation during the period 2000 to 2017

4.5 INTENSITY INDICES

Before making a detailed study about the commodity trade potential between India and the ASEAN, it would be in the fitness of things to make a careful analysis on the growth of the export intensity and import intensity trade between the two. According to the "natural trading partner theory" trade between countries who are neighbours and proximity to each other benefit from the FTAs (Krugman, 1991). Hence, ASEAN countries being closer to India from a distance point of view, tend to trade more with their partners. The Intensity Indices of "Export Intensity Index (XII)" and the "Import Intensity Index (MII)" is given in Table 4.6 and Table. 4.7 respectively. The Modified Export Intensity Index (E'II)

Table 4.6 Export Intensity Index of India with the ASEAN Nations (EII) 2000-2017

Year	Singapore	Indonesia	Malaysia	Philippines	Thailand	Laos	Brunei Darusallam	Cambodia	Vietnam	Mynamar
2000	0.659	-	0.692	0.406	0.959	0.622	0.232	0.424	1.472	1.694
2001	0.841	-	1.07	0.576	1.06	0.886	0.185	0.504	1.459	2.341
2002	1.125	-	0.876	1.08	1.145	0.29	0.28	0.665	1.534	2.537
2003	1.248	1.693	0.822	0.654	0.943	0.064	0.26	0.675	1.443	2.348
2004	1.804	1.383	0.821	0.572	0.764	0.078	0.263	0.406	1.396	2.856
2005	2.083	1.168	0.707	0.623	0.677	0.391	0.2	0.371	1.233	2.449
2006	1.85	1.364	0.647	0.635	0.712	0.1	1.536	0.59	1.283	2.189
2007	1.577	1.051	0.739	0.496	0.737	0.091	0.142	0.44	1.198	1.859
2008	1.655	1.068	0.969	0.528	0.662	0.096	0.377	0.376	1.259	1.966
2009	1.472	1.37	1.27	0.555	0.672	0.495	0.521	0.314	1.225	1.546
2010	1.451	1.39	0.892	0.439	0.563	0.11	0.321	0.269	1.17	1.316
2011	1.924	1.415	0.771	0.458	0.551	0.135	6.157	0.311	1.204	1.486
2012	1.599	1.233	0.726	0.477	0.628	0.196	0.236	0.326	1.191	1.407
2013	1.62	1.136	0.977	0.592	0.733	0.375	0.211	0.358	1.538	1.593
2014	1.042	0.902	0.788	0.512	0.628	0.341	0.25	0.375	1.398	1.506
2015	1.014	0.735	0.982	0.495	0.627	0.3	0.244	0.337	1.065	1.461
2016	0.993	0.822	0.874	0.5	0.604	0.147	0.432	0.246	1.1	1.927
2017	1.363	1.041	1.196	0.724	0.691	0.204	0.789	0.373	1.708	2.47
Average	1.407	1.185	0.879	0.573	0.742	0.273	0.702	0.409	1.326	1.942

Source: Author's calculation based on data extracted from unctad.org

which verifies the Export Intensity Index (XII) is presented in the Table. 4.8. Inferences from the earlier studies on the trade structures between the nations present that both the nations have much to offer each other and the trade is intensifying among nations. In this context, the sections present the analysis of the export intensity and import intensity indices between the nations.

4.5.1 India's "Export Intensity Indices" with the ASEAN

Table 4.6 lists India's export intensity with the ASEAN countries for the years 2000 to 2017. The Export Intensity Index (XII) value is greater than 1 for countries Singapore, Indonesia, Vietnam and Myanmar. The "Export Intensity Index" of India with Singapore presents an average XII index which is 1.40. Singapore is a substantial trade partner to India. India also ranks 10th among Singapore's trade partners. India remained a net exporter to Singapore and with contributing about 2.3% in total international trade of Singapore during 2017. The country's XII values with Singapore has been higher than one since the year 2000 and has been greater than one for all the years. Indonesia too emerged as a prominent export destination for India and the export intensity of trade is higher than one for all the years except for the year 2014, 2015 and the year 2016. Exports amounted to US$ 3 billion with India during the year 2017. With India's "CLMV (Cambodia, Lao PDR, Myanmar and Vietnam)" initiative taken up by the country, the XII of India with Vietnam has been consistently progressing with average XII of Vietnam and Myanmar at 1.32 and 1.94 respectively.

The "Export Intensity Index" of India with Malaysia presented that Malaysia has developed as a significant export destination for India. India has become 10th largest trading partner to Malaysia, with the XII of India with Malaysia being 1.196 during the year 2017 and with an average XII of 0.878. The XII of India with the Philippines has been consistently growing, and average XII is 0.573. Thailand intimal XII values have been above one for the years 2001 and 2002, and after that, there was a decline due to the fierce competition of the export market from China. There is a gradual growing intensity of trade exports of India with Brunei, and average XII is 0.702. The average XII with Cambodia and Lao PDR is 0.408 and 0.273, which are the lowest among the ASEAN group (Chart. 4.3).

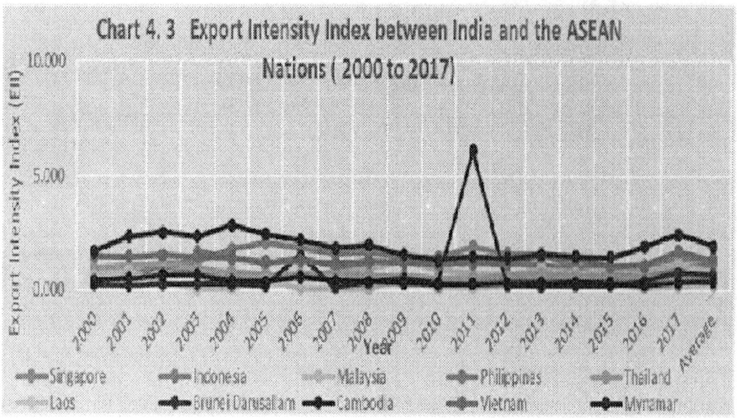

Source: Chart based on Table 4.6.

The trends of XII of India with the ASEAN presented that exports of India with the ASEAN have been more than one considering its pattern of trade with the other countries. The XII of ASEAN is more significant than one since its exports to India are higher than imports from India, which could be analyzed from the below section.

4.5.2 India's Import Intensity Indices with the ASEAN

Table 4.7 and Chart. 4.4 presents Import Intensity Indices of India with the countries of ASEAN. India's imports from less developed countries of ASEAN are

Table 4.7 Import Intensity Index of India with the ASEAN Nations (MII) 2000-2017

Year	*Singapore*	*Indonesia*	*Malaysia*	*Philippines*	*Thailand*	*Laos*	*Brunei Darussalam*	*Cambodia*	*Vietnam*	*Myanmar*
2000	2.42		2.607	0.264	0.982		0.00572	0.073	0.324	20.69
2001	2.63		2.425	0.361	1.084		1.09253	0.06	0.328	25.78
2002	2.33		2.412	0.442	0.844	0.03	0.01419	0.034	0.345	21.12
2003	2.06	3.77	2.804	0.4	0.978	0.045	1.3044	0.011	0.22	21.16
2004	1.98	3.84	2.431	0.393	1.029	0.018	3.38403	0.008	0.336	19.89
2005	1.95	3.32	2.228	0.359	1.193	0.01	2.07111	0.012	0.337	13.84
2006	1.81	2.67	2.343	0.258	1.013	0.02	3.019	0.021	0.288	12.22
2007	1.76	2.52	2.033	0.26	0.984	0.006	2.08277	0.022	0.216	8.452
2008	1.63	2.68	2.023	0.242	0.93	0.015	2.35685	0.045	0.331	7.696
2009	1.49	3.31	1.634	0.365	1.02	0.006	4.27759	0.053	0.391	9.533
2010	1.35	2.86	1.452	0.361	0.994	0.266	1.60049	0.07	0.634	5.534
2011	1.16	2.86	1.713	0.369	0.978	0.669	2.793	0.066	0.682	5.051
2012	0.91	2.82	1.75	0.316	0.959	1.258	3.09919	0.049	0.658	9.301
2013	0.98	3.38	1.666	0.271	1.017	1.084	3.08902	0.066	0.861	4.713
2014	0.97	3.39	1.925	0.245	1.077	0.511	3.93052	0.078	0.762	4.239
2015	1.17	3.81	1.989	0.339	1.135	1.28	4.17021	0.138	0.712	3.985
2016	1.13	3.57	1.998	0.319	1.129	1.792	4.07029	0.151	0.789	4.156
2017	0.57	2.91	1.21	0.368	0.858	1.535	2.49053	0.128	1.138	1.745
Average	1.57	3.18	2.036	0.33	1.011	0.534	2.49175	0.06	0.52	11.06

Source: "Author's calculation based on data extracted from unctad.org."

smaller as Import intensity Index was low with Lao PDR and Cambodia. Average Import Intensity Index (MII) of Cambodia (0.602), Laos (0.534). Low imports were also observed with the Philippines and Vietnam with import intensity lower than 1. The average Import Intensity Index (MII) of the Philippines and Cambodia at 0.329 and 0.060, respectively. India's MII was low with Thailand for an extended period, but it has shown considerable improvement after both the countries have signed a free trade agreement. Imports of India from ASEAN historically bound to Malaysia and Singapore. Singapore has emerged as a famous import destination, and the average MII is 1.572 and Malaysia with 2.035. India's MII with Myanmar is significantly high, could be due to Myanmar's geographical proximity to India's northeastern states. The reason for such high import intensity also could be that Myanmar's imports from other countries are low, which is 20.686 in the year 2000 and decline during the post subprime crisis 2007 and 2008 and after that, there was a gradual decline, but overall MII is above 1.

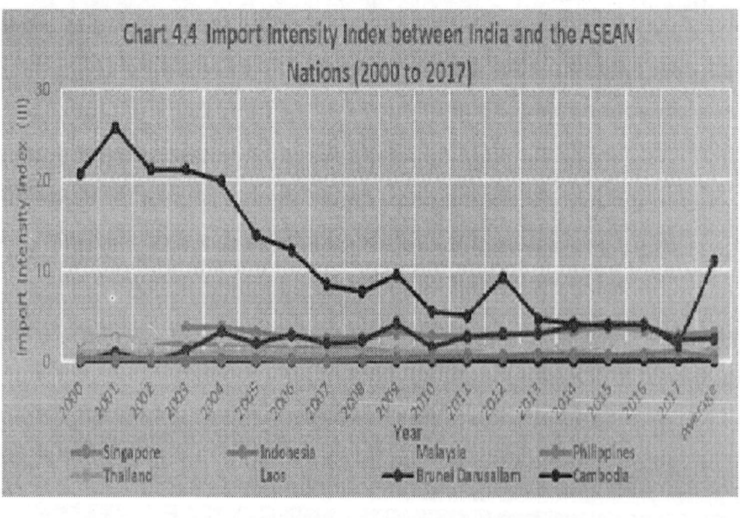

Chart 4.4 Import Intensity Index between India and the ASEAN Nations (2000 to 2017)

Source: Chart based on Table 4.6.

The Chart of 4.4 shows the Import Intensity Index values of India's with the ASEAN nations. 6 among 10 nations present an intensity index about one and 4 nations present an index below one. Also, a growing import intensity index could be observed with many of the countries. India's "Look East Policy" Strategy and further strengthening with the "Act East Policy" are presented over a growing intensity of import trade with the ASEAN countries.

4.5.3 India's "Modified Export Intensity Index" of India with the ASEAN Nations (X'II)

The Modified Export Intensity Index (X'II) value presents the "Modified Export Intensity Index" of India with the ASEAN countries. For the countries which have lower integration of trade in terms of exports with the other countries in the world the values of "Export Intensity Index (XII)" and the value of "Modified Trade Intensity Index (X'II)" is similar. The higher values of the Modified Trade Intensity Index (X'II) presents a greater integration of the nation with the outside world when compared to the countries under partnership. Table. 4.8 shows the "Modified Trade Intensity Index (X'II)" of India with the ASEAN countries. Chart 4.5 presents a comparison of "Export Intensity Index" and the "Modified Export Intensity" indices for India's trade with the ASEAN countries.

The average "Modified Export Intensity Index" of India with the ASEAN nations presents that the values of X'II is above 1 for Singapore, Indonesia, Vietnam, Myanmar and ASEAN -10 also the average X'II presents a value which is higher than 1 indicating a higher bilateral trade flow, given the relevance of ASEAN's trade in the world trade. It is also seen that the Singapore Modified Export Intensity Index is 0.657 during the initial period of 2000, and this has grown to 1.372 during the year 2017,

Table. 4.8 Modified Export Intensity Index of India with the ASEAN Nations (X'II) 2000-2017

Year	Singapore	Indonesia	Malaysia	Philippines	Thailand	Laos PDI	Brunei Darus	Cambodia	Vietnam	Mynamar	ASEAN 10
2000	0.657		0.69	0.404	0.959	0.62	0.231	0.422	1.478	1.705	0.723
2001	0.84		1.071	0.574	1.06	0.885	0.183	0.502	1.466	2.374	0.914
2002	1.127		0.875	1.081	1.147	0.288	0.278	0.663	1.543	2.581	1.047
2003	1.252	1.706	0.821	0.651	0.942	0.064	0.257	0.673	1.451	2.384	1.104
2004	1.823	1.39	0.819	0.569	0.762	0.077	0.261	0.403	1.403	2.925	1.169
2005	2.117	1.171	0.704	0.62	0.674	0.388	0.197	0.367	1.237	2.504	1.161
2006	1.875	1.372	0.643	0.631	0.709	0.099	1.549	0.586	1.289	2.232	1.13
2007	1.593	1.052	0.735	0.492	0.733	0.089	0.14	0.436	1.202	1.887	1.04
2008	1.676	1.069	0.968	0.523	0.657	0.094	0.373	0.371	1.266	2.003	1.095
2009	1.487	1.381	1.278	0.55	0.667	0.49	0.516	0.309	1.231	1.564	1.19
2010	1.466	1.402	0.89	0.433	0.558	0.108	0.316	0.264	1.175	1.326	1.061
2011	1.969	1.43	0.767	0.452	0.545	0.132	7.066	0.305	1.211	1.504	1.235
2012	1.623	1.24	0.721	0.471	0.623	0.192	0.231	0.321	1.197	1.422	1.104
2013	1.645	1.14	0.976	0.586	0.728	0.369	0.207	0.353	1.559	1.617	1.253
2014	1.043	0.899	0.784	0.505	0.622	0.335	0.245	0.369	1.413	1.527	0.987
2015	1.014	0.73	0.981	0.488	0.621	0.294	0.239	0.332	1.067	1.479	0.928
2016	0.993	0.818	0.871	0.493	0.597	0.144	0.426	0.241	1.103	1.978	0.899
2017	1.372	1.041	1.2	0.721	0.687	0.202	0.787	0.369	1.729	2.534	1.186
Average	1.421	1.19	0.878	0.569	0.738	0.27	0.75	0.405	1.334	1.975	1.068

Source: Author's calculation based on data extracted from unctad.org

the average X'II value is 1.421. The Export Intensity Index (XII) value of India with Singapore is 0.659 during the year 2000, and this has increased to 1.362 during the year 2017 and average XII value is at 1.40, given the importance of Singapore as the 10 largest export destination for India, there is a minimal difference between the values of XII and X'II. Though Indonesia was a prominent export destination for India, the trade share of the country compared with Singapore is less, the Modified X'II value for the year 2003 is 1.706, and the values steadily declined to 1.041 during the year 2017. If these are compared with the XII values which were 1.692 during the year 2003 and this was 1.040 during the year 2017 presenting higher integration of India with remaining countries. The Modified Export Intensity Index values of Philippines present that till the year 2009 the XII and the X'II values were similar with slight variations but with the experience of post-crisis scenario and signing of India –ASEAN FTA the Modified Export Intensity values during the year, India's integration with other ASEAN members rose like Myanmar and Vietnam resulting in variation of X'II. The Modified Export Intensity Index of India with Thailand is 0.959 in the year 2000, and this has declined to 0.687 during the year 2017. The X'II of India with Thailand for the year 2017 has been 0.690. Modified Export Intensity Index values of India with Lao PDR, Brunei and Cambodia have been small given the sizes of the economies. Vietnam and Myanmar XII and X'II values has been on rise and above 1. The X'II value during the year 2000 for Myanmar is 1.705., and this has gradually risen to 2.534 during the year 2017. The difference between the XII and X'II is significant that the XII value of India with Myanmar during the year 200 is 1.693, and this rose to 2.470 during the year 2017. The XII of Vietnam during the year 2000 is 1.471, and this gradually rose to 1.707 during the year 2017, compared to the X'II which is 1.705 during the year 2000, and this rose to 2.534.

The overall summary of the "Export Intensity Index" and "Modified Export Intensity Index" analysis presents that India's export share is gradually on rising and intensity is growing with the ASEAN nations, but there is a need to diversify to other export destinations and increase the volume of trade. The Make in India Campaign and Start-Up initiatives has popped up at the right time by the government to boost the export volumes of the country.

Chart 4.5 Export Intensity Index (XII) and Modefiied Export Intensity Index (X'II) of India with the ASEAN Nations (2000-2017)

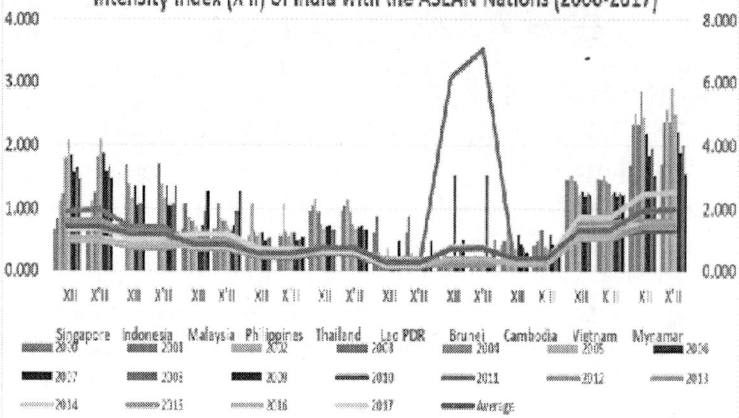

4.6 MAJOR FINDINGS OF THE CHAPTER

1. With the developments of the Indo-ASEAN trade relations since 1997 and the initiation of India's "Look East Policy" strategy and further up-gradation to the "Act East Policy" the trade intensity of India, the export and import intensity of trade with the ASEAN nations have been rising. Especially the current chapter finds that the countries of Vietnam, Myanmar, Brunei has been on the rise along with the other prominent trade partners of India viz. Singapore, Indonesia, Malaysia and Thailand.

2. The "Trade Openness Index" of India with the ASEAN nations presents that India's "Trade Openness Index" value has been low compared with the ASEAN countries, which plays a prominent role impacting the trade volumes.
3. The trade (export and import) share of ASEAN countries when compared with India, USA and China, presents a growing share of trade volumes with China replacing the USA. The trade share of India remains low, but on an increasing trajectory.
4. The values of "Export Intensity Index (XII)" and "Import Intensity Index (MII)" presents a gradual increasing trend especially after, the year 2010, Free Trade Agreement (FTA) between both the economies was signed.
5. The Modified Trade Intensity values with respect to India with the ASEAN countries remained almost the same till the year 2009, but owing to the post-crisis strategies adopted by countries and India's new Foreign trade policies accelerating and diversifying the trade with respect of the world, there was a gradual rise exhibiting an improvement in the trade volume of India with the rest of the world. The CLMV strategy followed by India with respect to "Cambodia, Laos, Myanmar and Vietnam" played a marked role in intensifying the trade with these countries which could be observed in the increasing intensity of trade values with these countries.
6. The values of "Trade Intensity Index" and "Modified Trade Intensity Index" of ASEAN with India have revealed a fluctuating trend for the period under study, but for most of the years, they were more than one revealing a higher intensity in trade between India and the ASEAN.

4.7. CONCLUSION

The trade with ASEAN countries for India has been increasing since 1980, both as markets for India's non-traditional exports and more so as sources of India's imports. ASEAN as a region and most of its founding members have displayed greater dynamism. The share of ASEAN in global exports increased twice between 1980 to 2017. These countries, therefore, hold immense opportunity for increasing trade with India. This is evident from the results of growing intensities of trade between them as a result of persuasion of India by the "Look East Policy". The up-gradation of "Look East Policy" to the "Act East Policy" and new CLMV strategy towards Asian countries and diversifying the foreign trade policy to include new import and export partners have intensified and accelerated India's volume of trade. The commodity trade potential of India and the ASEAN member states, which plays a significant role in increasing the trade relations are reviewed in the next chapter.

5

India's Revealed Comparative Advantage: An Analysis

India and the ASEAN (Association of Southeast Asian Nations) passed through a long journey interspersed with several achievements to reach the year 2017. India and ASEAN have completed 25 years of engagement as partners. India and the ASEAN recognize each other's role in the development of the region and shaping its future. In pursuit of this objective, India started with "Look East Policy" and then to "Act East Policy" in 2014. The ASEAN-India combinedly as one among the large trade blocs in the world with a combined population of 180 crores. In terms of the trading partnership, ASEAN occupies the fourth-largest position for India, and it accounts for 10.6 per cent of its total trade of India. India occupies 7th position in ASEAN's trade, and there are perfect complementarities between service economy of India and manufacturing-oriented ASEAN.

The Asia-Pacific region is spearheading the global economy today towards growth and dynamism. The Asia-Pacific is among the growing most region of the world today. In a groundbreaking achievement towards greater integration in Asian economies, the "ASEAN Economic

Community" (AEC) was incorporated in 2015 as it aims to consolidate diverse economies of Southeast Asia into a single economic entity. Indian Government had set forth several actions to enhance strategic relations and partnership with the countries in Southeast Asia. For instance, India has initiated CLMV project to focus on the countries namely "Cambodia, Laos, Myanmar, and Vietnam" and to extend the highway connecting these countries, the "East-West Economic Corridor" (EWEC). Engaging with private companies has also been one of the critical areas of focus for the two sides. "The ASEAN India-Business Council (AIBC)" was started during March 2003 to provide an inclusive forum to organizations in private sector in India as well as in ASEAN countries, for business networking has also been one of the crucial steps to boost the trade relations.

India and ASEAN have targeted to reach a minimum US$ 200 billion in the bilateral trade by 2022 from US$ 71 billion during the year 2016-17. Despite an impressive trajectory of trade relations between the two nations, further growth is possible through the economic inclusion of India into the Asian production value chains. In this background, the chapter aims to explore the comparative advantage of commodity trade between India and the ASEAN nations and identify India's trade specialization through Lafay's index. This chapter has six sections. Section I presents the objectives of the chapter, Methodology of the chapter is given in Section II. Section III analyzes the "Revealed Comparative Advantage Index" (RCA) about commodity trade between India and ASEAN nations, and this is verified through the Stability index. Section IV details India's commodity trade possibilities using Lafay's index. Section V presents the major findings of the chapter and the last section Section.VI presents the conclusions of the chapter.

5.1. OBJECTIVES OF THE STUDY

- To identify the commodity trade potential between India and the ASEAN, which could increase the trade relation between the partners by using various indices of RXA, RMA, RTA, and B(beta)values.
- To further assess the stability of these indices using the B values.
- To identify India's trade specialization through Lafay's index.
- To review the avenues of trade opportunities and to appraise the possibilities of trade between India and the ASEAN member states taken for study.

5.2. DATABASE AND METHODOLOGY

In this chapter, the author has used both descriptive and analytical methods of research. The chapter's study is presented based on secondary data taken from the research papers, journals, periodicals, books, databases such as UNCTAD, IMF, Ministry of Finance of Government of India, Ministry of Commerce and Industry. The data includes time-series data of imports and exports from 2008 to 2017. Relevant statistical techniques given in SPSS 16.0 are used to analyze the data to make an accurate and scientific study and to derive logical findings. The "Revealed Comparative Advantage" (RCA), is the most prevalent concept for analyzing the trade data. Balassa initially propounded RCA in 1965, and later economists have modified the basic RCA measure, and now several RCA measures are available in the literature. There is some variation of RCA measure which is aimed at measuring the index at global level, and some of them limit the analysis only to the partners in bilateral trade. As the context is to measure the competitiveness of Indian exports concerning ASEAN countries, the researcher has calculated RCAs with the ASEAN taking total trade flows instead of bilateral trade flows.

5.2.1 Calculation of Revealed Comparative Advantage

The approach of "Revealed Comparative Advantage (RCA)" is based on traditional theories of international trade. The first "**RCA index**", theorized by Balassa (1965), can be written as:

"B= $(x_{ij}/x_{it}/\ x_{nj}/x_{nt})$

Where x represents exports, 'i' is a country, 'j' is a commodity, 't' is a set of commodities and 'n' is a set of countries". B is derived from the patterns of trade between two countries; it calculates the "country's exports of a product in relation to its total exports and the corresponding exports of a group of countries", e.g., the ASEAN. "If B>1, then a comparative advantage is revealed". (Balassa, 1965)

Vollrath (1991) has given "three alternative measures of revealed comparative advantage", based on "Analyses of International Competitiveness in Agriculture" (Vollrath, 1987 and 1989; and Vollrath and Vo, 1990). One of these alternatives is "***Relative Trade Advantage*** (RTA)", which considers imports as well as exports. RTA "is the difference between **Relative Export Advantage** (RXA) and **Relative Import Advantage** (RMA):

$$RTA= RXA-RMA$$

Where,

$$RXA=B$$

and

$$RMA= (m_{ij}/m_{it})/(m_{nj}/m_{nt})$$

Where 'm' represents imports. Thus,

$$RTA= \left[\left(\frac{xij}{xit}\right)/\left(\frac{xnj}{xnt}\right)\right] - \left[\left(\frac{mij}{mit}\right)/\left(\frac{mnj}{mnt}\right)\right]"$$

(Eiteljorge and Hartmann, 1999)

Vollrath's "second measure is the log of the RTA (In RXA)". The third measure "Revealed Competitiveness (RC)" which is defined as:

"*RC= In RXA-In RMA.*"

By taking these "two indices in logarithmic form, they become symmetric through the origin. Positive values of RTA, lnRXA and RC reveal a comparative/competitive advantage" (Volrath, 1991)

5.2.2 The Lafay's Index: Measuring Trade Specialization

"Index of *Revealed Comparative Advantage* (RCA)" of Balassa gives observational inputs to the "theory of comparative advantage" proposed by David Ricardo. The index compares the design of the export of a country with global exports structure and thus it is concerned with data on exports only. If high-level disaggregation is used for the analysis, there is a likelihood of missing out on valuable information. Lafay's (1992) *index* is an improved version after "Balassa RCA index" which also considers the imports. By using "Lafay's Index", trade specialization of a country for a specific product is defined as the difference between exports and imports of that product to the difference between total exports and imports of a country (the Trade balance), by applying a weightage equal to the product's share in total trade. "Lafay's index" captures the "Intra-Industry Trade" movements, which became apparent in many industries. An advantage in using "Lafay's revealed comparative advantage index" (LFI) is that "it can control for distortions due to the macroeconomic fluctuations" (Lafay, 1992). Taking on from the literature on trade (e.g., Alessandrini et al. 2011), we analyze using "Lafay's index" (Lafay, 1992) and by applying the below-given formula.

"(LFI Formula as proposed by Bugamelli, 2001)

$$LFI^i_j = 100\left(\frac{x^i_j - m^i_j}{x^i_j + m^i_j} - \frac{\sum_{j=1}^{N}\left(x^i_j - m^i_j\right)}{\sum_{j=1}^{N}\left(x^i_j + m^i_j\right)}\right)\frac{x^i_j + m^i_j}{\sum_{j=1}^{N}\left(x^i_j + m^i_j\right)}$$

where

LFIj: Lafay index of product *j*,

xj: Exports of product *j* towards the rest of the world,

mj: Imports of product *j* from the rest of the world,

N: Number of traded goods.

According to this index, the comparative advantage for the country under investigation in product *j* is the deviation of the product *j* normalized trade balance from the overall normalized trade balance. Thus, the sum of *LFI* across *j* for any year must by construction be equal to zero, i.e., 1

As the index measures each group's contribution to the overall normalized trade balance, the following relation holds: the positive value of the *LFI* indicates comparative advantages in a given item and the higher the value, the higher the degree of specialization, with the sector making a bigger contribution to the trade balance. On the contrary, negative value implies reliance on imports." (Bugamelli, 2001)

5.3 DATA AND EMPIRICAL FINDINGS

5.3.1 Revealed Comparative Advantage of India with the ASEAN

India set out on "Look East policy" in 1991 for increasing trade participation with East Asian countries. Regular interaction is maintained with the ASEAN countries through Summit level meetings, Ministerial engagements, and official interactions to fulfil the economic framework of "Look East Policy". The "Look East Polic"' has been rechristened as "Act East Policy" during the year 2014. The regional co-operation can open fresh possibilities for increased pace of equitable growth for the participant countries, which is evident from the complementarities that exist between the nations. To examine the possibilities of co-operation - the four RCA indices enumerated above are calculated for India's trade with ASEAN for the 10 country grouping over a ten year period of time from 2008 to 2017, for 7 specific product categories and 37 product groups (as per Lemer's Aggregation Scheme at "Standard Industrial Trade Classification (SITC)" and the data was obtained from UNCTAD database. The complete sample encompasses 37 product groups and includes trade flows in each of the ten years. Annual RCA indices are calculated from the UNCTAD database.

The summary calculations ("mean and coefficient of variation") for all the 4 RCA indices ("Balassa Index' B', Relative Trade Advantage' RTA,' Relative Export Advantage' RXA,' Relative Import Advantage 'RMA'"), are given in **Table. 5.1**. The pattern shows similarity for all 4 indices exhibiting "Revealed Comparative Advantage"; for 37 **specific product groups** (Appendix.1) under the 7 categories.

Table 5.1 Revealed Comparative Advantages of India with the ASEAN by Product Group (2008-2017)

Revealed Comparative Advantage:	Mean				Coefficient of Variation (percent)			
	B	RTA	ln RXA	RC	B	RTA	ln RXA	RC
	>1	>0	>0	>0				
Food and Live Animals								
Live animals other than animals of division 03	0.23	**0.18**	-0.69	0.57	52.42	72.3	-33.92	51.12
Meat and meat preparations	0	0	-3.66	-1.24	141.3	-73.34	-15.45	-57.29
Dairy products and birds' eggs	**1.96**	**0.91**	-0.15	**1.36**	75.12	81.81	-255.95	50.55
Fish, crustaceans, mollusks, and preparations thereof	0.25	**0.1**	-0.68	**0.19**	55.35	147.71	-40.98	162.33
Cereals and cereal preparations	**17.5**	**17.4**	**1.21**	**2.96**	37.02	37.05	13.41	5.8
Vegetables and fruits	**1.44**	-2.39	**0.15**	-0.43	15.81	-22.39	44.28	-20.44
Sugar, sugar preparations and honey	**7.45**	**6.36**	**0.76**	**0.92**	54.57	77.56	53.79	89.89
Coffee, tea, cocoa, spices, and manufactures thereof	**2.15**	**1.78**	**0.32**	**0.77**	30.06	34.36	37.98	18.59
Feedstuff for animals (excluding unmilled cereals)	**5.68**	**5.54**	**0.69**	**1.56**	45.34	46.83	38.89	22.43
Miscellaneous edible products and preparations	0.26	**0.17**	-0.59	**0.46**	14.34	24.7	-10	19.73
Beverages and Tobacco								
Beverages	0.29	**0.08**	-0.54	**0.15**	8.797	53.48	-7.29	66.40
Tobacco and tobacco manufacture	**8.89**	**8.83**	**0.94**	**2.2**	17.53	17.6	8.83	4.95
Mineral Fuels, Lubricants and Related Materials:								
Coal, coke and briquettes	**24.9**	**22**	**1.28**	**0.84**	71.46	82.24	27.7	47.04
Petroleum, petroleum products and related materials	**1.96**	-2.53	**-0.04**	-0.5	30.88	-69.87	-406.87	-45.72
Gas, natural and manufactured	0.01	-1.4	-2.25	-2.39	90.48	-22.28	-18.94	-18.93
Electric current	0.02	-0.22		**1.16**	307.3			212.19

Revealed Comparative Advanrage:	Mean				Coefficient of Variation (percent)			
	B	RTA	In RXA	RC	B	RTA	In RXA	RC
	>1	>0	>0	>0				
Chemicals and Related Products n.e.s:								
Organic chemicals	**1.75**	**5.65**	**0.78**	**0.77**	46.35	55.63	26.75	31.59
Inorganic chemicals	**1.41**	-1.56	**0.03**	-0.38	27.9	-49.22	338.87	-35.74
Dyeing, tanning and coloring materials	0.01	0.6	**0.56**	**0.08**	16.55	112.41	12.81	112.20
Medicinal and pharmaceutical products	**17.4**	**6.87**	**0.86**	**1.15**	19.83	21.24	10.71	9.37
Essential oils for perfume materials and cleaning preparations	0.57	**2.04**	**0.4**	**0.7**	17.79	21.86	19.23	11.70
Fertilizers other than group 272	0.33	-4.08	-0.58	-1.21	56.16	-19.89	-33.45	-17.86
Manufactured Goods								
Leather, leather manufactures and dressed furskins	**1.12**	**4.08**	**0.73**	**0.59**	25.73	33.99	14.57	20.18
Rubber manufactures, n.e.s.	0.27	0.64	**0.11**	**0.29**	20.08	51.79	80.14	46.43
Cork and wood manufactures (excluding furniture)	0.17	**2.14**	**0.47**	**0.55**	25.06	45.36	26.34	47.80
Paper and paper manufactures	0.44	-1.17	-2.51	-2.58	65.41	-11.03	-19.87	-19.67
Textile yarn and related products	**2.17**	**2.39**	**0.59**	**0.39**	19.3	34.57	15.17	28.92
Iron and steel	**3.41**	**1.48**	**0.36**	**0.4**	32.61	52.01	37.06	33.19
Machinery and Transport Equipment								
Specialised machinery	**1.42**	**-0.02**	**-0.33**	**-0**	32.12	-795.5	-41.52	-397.63
Telecommunication and sound recording apparatus	**1.21**	-1.03	-0.64	-0.77	82.5	-35.82	-62.96	-53.57
Electrical Machinery, Apparatus and Appliances, n.e.s.	0.23	-0.3	-0.65	-0.37	18.58	-22.33	-12.55	-13.29
Road vehicles	0.41	**12.5**	**1.03**	**2.56**	56.62	56.76	26.28	12.77
Other transport equipment	**4.15**	**2.22**	**0.37**	**1.28**	16.21	18.48	19.78	18.78
Miscellaneous Manufactured Articles								
Furniture and parts thereof	0.47	-0.75	-0.65	-0.64	18.58	-16.78	-12.55	-10.15
Travel goods, handbags, etc.	**2.76**	**0.35**	-0.14	**0.29**	14.67	28.24	-45.29	34.49
Footwear	**1.38**	**1.69**	**0.36**	**0.56**	18.76	29.19	22.4	23.24
Professional and scientific instruments, n.e.s.	0.54	-0.61	-0.32	-0.35	12.18	-18.46	-16.02	-13.64

Source: Author's calculation based on SITC-level data from www.unctad.org

Note: Revealed Comparative Advantage index values are shown in bold.

From the above Table, the "Relative Trade Advantage" is evident in 22 product groups, details given in Appendix 2. These product groups have the potential to become the largest part of the export basket for India's trade with ASEAN since RTA is greater than 1 for these product groups. For 20 commodities, "In RXA (Relative Export Advantage)" has returned value more than 1 giving the details of products where India has greater participation with ASEAN. (Appendix.3). The "Revealed Competitiveness" (RC) is greater than 1 for 24 commodities as given in the Appendix. 4. Table 5.2 gives a summary of the mean and coefficient of variation for the 4 indices used in the analysis. The "Coefficient of Variation tested the stability of the indices", and as it was relatively lower, indices were found to be stable during the 10 years.

When the RCA indices with respect to B Value, RTA, In RXA and RC are considered it is quite evident that Indian exports have a comparative advantage with at least 26 commodities on an average. These are sectors that the country can focus on tapping the untapped potential with its East Asian Neighbors.

5.3.2: Stability of Revealed Comparative Advantage

The *coefficients of variation* given in Table. 5.2 suggests that the indices of RCA were quite steady throughout the period 2008-2017. In order to inspect this further, the indices were analyzed by applying stability indicating measures. "A simple indicator of stability is the relative importance of those products which reveal a comparative advantage during the period 't' but a disadvantage in the period t+1 or vice-versa, i.e., a Revealed Comparative Disadvantage (RCD) in 't' and an RCA in t+1" (Hoekman and Djankov,1997). Some product categories where India had RCA (Revealed Comparative Advantage) in the year 2008 but an RCD (Revealed Comparative Disadvantage) in the year 2017 accounted between 57 % and 47 % of the combined value of the 37 commodities (Table 5.2). For some product groups, a 'switch' is observed in the opposite way– an RCD in the year 2008 but RCA in the year 2017 were prevailing a bit more but yet constituted about 52 % of the total value of the commodities in either of these years as presented in the below Table (Table.5.3). It shows that the India's RCA has not changed much during the study period in its basic structure.

Table 5.2 Percentage Share of Product Groups where:

Index	RCA2008	and	RCD 2017	RCD2008	and	RCA2017
	2008		2017	2008		2017
B	57.89		47.37	42.11		52.63
RTA	60.53		39.47	39.474		60.53
In RXA	57.89		50	42.11		50
RC	60.53		39.47	39.474		60.526

Source: Authors' calculations based on SITC Rev.3 data

Following Hinloopen and Van Marrewijk (2001), the changes in distribution of Balassa Index could be seen in Table 5.3, and it shows that India's RCA has been fluctuating over time, as evidenced by the mean for the period 2008 is 4.096, and this saw a gradual decline to 3.575 by the year 2014 and 4.189 during the year 2017 and thereafter to 2.336 which means the distribution seemed to have shifted to the left, giving a higher fraction of indices with lower value. The illustration for this phenomenon is given in Table.5.3. The mean value of the B index reduced by 50 per cent over time, and the maximum value also saw a decline since the year 2008 (23.391) to 13.202 by the year 2018 presenting a declining trend in the RCA Index. Moreover, in the year 2008, 31.58 percent of the 'B' values were less than 3 and

Table 5.3 The Distribution of Balassa Index, 'B' Value

Summary Statistics	2008	2009	2010	2011	2012	2013	2014	2015	2016	2017	2018
Mean	4.095	4.016	3.278	4.401	3.801	3.888	3.575	3.035	2.505	4.189	2.336
Maximum	23.391	20.289	18.873	24.42	26.081	47.237	29.853	19.995	13.964	16.363	13.202
Percent of B Index											
<1	57.895	52.632	57.895	57.895	55.263	55.263	52.632	55.263	52.632	50	52.632
<2	39.474	44.737	39.474	42.105	36.842	42.105	39.474	44.737	42.105	39.474	34.211
<3	31.579	39.474	34.211	28.947	28.947	31.579	31.579	31.579	28.947	28.947	23.684
<4	21.053	26.316	23.684	23.684	23.684	26.316	26.316	23.684	21.053	23.684	18.421

Source: Authors' calculations based on SITC Rev.3 data

remained stable at 31.579 by 2013 and later declined to 23.684 in the year 2018. 21.053 per cent of the B value is less than 4 in 2008, and this increased to 26.31 per cent in the year 2013 and reduced to 18.421 per cent by the year 2018. The fall in B index demonstrates the weakening of RCA of India coincides with the fall in India's exports to ASEAN countries. This could be due to a decline as a result of the reduction in prices due to the slump in the world economy along with competition from other Asian countries, including China.

5.4 AN ANALYSIS OF LAFAY'S INDEX OF INDIA AND ASEAN

India and the ASEAN countries trade specialization patterns have been calculated using the Lafay's index LFI equation mentioned in the methodology section for the period .2011 to 2017 for the 57 commodity category under 7 distinct product group as per the Leamer's Aggregation scheme. The analysis has shown that, during the study period, 23 products have shown a negative LFI index where India does not have a comparative advantage, and it shows a lack of specialization. Among others these product groups: *Petroleum*: Oils from Petroleum and bitumen materials, *Raw Materials*: Crude Fertilizers, Base metal concentrates, Ores, Coke and Semi-cokes of coal, lignite, Liquefied and Non-liquefied natural gas, Waste and scrap of Non-ferrous base metals, *Food Products*: Wood manufactures, Cork manufactures, Pulp and Waste paper, *Tropical Agriculture*: Fixed Vegetable Fats & Oil, Chocolate, Food preparations with cocoa, Non-alcoholic beverages, *Animal Products*: Hides and Skins, *Cereals:*Worn Clothing, *Labour Intensive Manufactures:* Gold Non-monetary, Miscellaneous articles, *Machinery*: Office machines, Electrical Machinery & apparatus, *Chemicals:* Oxides, Halogen salts, Inorganic Chemical Elements, Extracts for dyeing and tanning, Synthetic tanning

Table 5.4 Lafay's Index Values for India with Positive Values

	2011	2012	2013	2014	2015	2016	2017	2011-17
Raw Materials								
Other crude minerals	-0.796	2.277	0.256	0.289	2.243	0.312	0.029	0.659
Forest products								
Paper and paperboard	0.142	1.028	0.099	0.094	0.822	0.275	-0.001	0.351
Tropical Agriculture								
Fruits and nuts (excluding oil nuts), fresh or dried	0.366	3.787	0.319	0.354	3.172	0.595	-0.008	1.226
Oil seeds & oleaginous fruits (incl. flour, n.e.s.)	0.013	0.275	0.017	0.059	0.541	0.069	0.004	0.14
Sugar, molasses, and honey	0.467	8.734	0.82	0.416	4.59	0.853	0.081	2.28
Coffee and coffee substitutes	0.261	3.536	0.314	0.291	2.679	0.453	0.035	1.081
Animal products								
Animal or veg. oils & fats, processed, n.e.s.; mixt.	0.053	0.81	0.056	0.075	0.701	0.134	0.007	0.262
Meat of bovine animals, fresh, chilled or frozen	0.879	10.967	1.159	1.733	18.589	2.486	0.214	5.147
Crude animal materials, n.e.s.	0.021	0.8	0.048	0.051	0.432	0.047	0.005	0.2
Fish, fresh (live or dead), chilled or frozen	0.38	3.907	0.358	0.377	3.583	0.489	0.049	1.306
Cereals								
Feeding stuff for animals (no unmilled cereals)	1.061	11.541	1.008	1.413	7.73	0.632	0.038	3.346
Tobacco, manufactured	0.084	0.937	0.084	0.09	1.013	0.178	0.019	0.343
Milk, cream and milk products (excluding butter, cheese)	0.023	-0.034	0.039	0.198	0.928	0.035	0.003	0.17

Labour Intensive Manufactures								
Mineral manufactures, n.e.s.	-0.181	0.757	0.092	0.105	1.057	0.206	0.014	0.293
Furniture & parts	0.264	2.625	0.274	0.323	3.307	0.585	0.05	1.061
Travel goods, handbags & similar containers	0.364	3.996	0.374	0.447	4.664	0.736	0.066	1.521
Articles of apparel, clothing access., excluding textile	0.304	3.871	0.357	0.432	4.223	0.622	0.053	1.409
Footwear	0.832	8.614	0.738	0.976	11.241	1.653	0.148	3.458
Capital Intensive Manufactures								
Leather	0.365	4.004	0.393	0.488	4.851	0.639	0.044	1.54
Rubber tyres, tyre treads or flaps & inner tubes	0.483	6.206	0.66	0.671	6.218	0.842	0.069	2.164
Textile yarn	2.047	19.318	1.875	2.479	21.69	3.253	0.228	7.27
Wire of iron or steel	0.121	1.574	0.11	0.114	1.09	0.158	0.011	0.454
Manufactures of base metal, n.e.s.	0.795	11.069	1.175	1.231	12.622	1.947	0.155	4.142
Sanitary, plumbing, heating fixtures, fittings, n.e.s.	0.003	0.573	0.025	0.03	0.258	0.05	0.005	0.135
Articles of apparel, textile fabrics, n.e.s.	1.423	15.561	1.521	1.944	21.731	3.556	0.329	6.581
Machinery								
Household type equipment, electrical or not, n.e.s.	0.06	0.526	0.034	0.055	0.827	0.156	0.008	0.241
Motor vehicles for the transport of persons	2.011	14.983	1.618	2.13	22.212	3.26	0.362	6.654
Chemicals								
Medicinal and pharmaceutical products, excluding 542	0.532	6.021	0.575	0.7	6.719	1.283	0.092	2.274
Essential oils, perfume &flavor materials	-0.21	2.561	0.33	0.313	2.602	0.453	0.035	0.869
Arms & ammunition	0.003	0.289	0.011	0.049	0.45	0.089	0.004	0.128

materials, Fertilizers, Miscellaneous chemical products, Sheets, Plates, Foils, Films, Strips of plastics. For *three* products, (i) Live Animals other than animals, (ii) Explosives and polytechnic products, (iii) Wool and other animal hair, explosives, and pyrotechnic products takes a zero value for the LFI index. The analysis shows that for these products, India has not acquired a comparative advantage. These findings through the LFI index suggest that India's export basket has undergone a diversification as presented in the most recent studies in the area. By comparing LFI values of Indian commodities with those of ASEAN countries, it is observed that India ranks first in case of 15 product groups. However, these 15 product categories were not occupying prominent share in imports of ASEAN countries. Also, it was observed that, for the remaining products, the LFI values for Indian commodities are lower than that of ASEAN countries. For a group of 33 products given in Table. 5.4, India's comparative advantage has been stable with positive LFI values. In the case of India, the LFI value for the Meat of bovine animals is 5.147 while the corresponding figures for Laos are 132.5, Thailand 120.36. In the case of Tropical Agriculture products where India's LFI for Fruits and nuts is 1.226 the LFI for Vietnam is 78.3, Cambodia is 69.8. Similarly, in the case of Edible vegetables, Animal products, feedstuff for animals, Footwear, Apparel, manufactures of base metals, textile yarn, and rubber tyres, though the values of LFI shown positive signs, when compared with ASEAN counterparts it is lower. If India has to utilize the advantage given by the *ASEAN India Free Trade Agreement,* India has to enhance the competitiveness of these sectors. As per the latest "ASEAN Statistical Yearbook (2018)", majority of imports of ASEAN include Mineral Fuels, Machinery & mechanical appliances, transport vehicles, electrical machinery and equipment, articles of iron and steel, and mineral wax. These products together accounted for 54% of total imports in the region during the year. When this is compared with India's RCA index values (Table 5.1) and Lafay's index (Table 5.4) except for two products Iron and Steel and Specialized machinery India's export potential was not evident for other products. The findings also suggest that India did not have a comparative advantage in the short run. The Statistical yearbook of ASEAN also presents that ASEAN countries are among leading exporters of the world in product segments such as light manufacturing products, agricultural products, for example, edible sugar, cereals, vegetable waxes, mineral fuels, organic chemicals, machinery & mechanical appliances, electrical machinery where India does not have comparative advantage. These results indicate a lower comparative advantage of India compared to that of ASEAN countries, and it is coinciding with lower trade balances of India with ASEAN. Therefore, this calls for India's diversification in commodity specialization pattern to match with the ASEAN counterparts. Also, the lack of comparative advantage for India in the products imported by ASEAN can pose a challenge in realizing the potential benefits that could be derived from ASEAN-India FTA in Goods.

5.5 MAJOR FINDINGS

- The "Relative Trade advantage (RTA)" is observed for 22 product categories with RTA>1. These commodities constitute potentially significant export products for India to trade with the ASEAN countries.
- "Revealed Export Advantage (RXA)' is observed in the case of 20 commodities, with RXA>1, and this illustrates India's greater integration with ASEAN countries in these products. Among these, the "Revealed Competitiveness (RC)" is >1 for 24 product categories.

- India is losing the comparative advantage, as illustrated by B index, coinciding with the decrease in the volume of India's exports to the ASEAN countries owing to a decline concerning the fall in commodity prices against due to the global economic slowdown.
- 23 products have shown a negative LFI index where India does not have a comparative advantage, and it shows a lack of specialization.
- For the remaining 33 products, India has maintained a comparative advantage, as shown by a positive value of the LFI. However, these products are not occupying a significant share in the ASEAN imports basket.
- The findings also suggest that India did not possess a comparative advantage in the short term.
- India should diversify its commodity specialization pattern to match with the ASEAN counterparts.
- Also, India's lack of comparative advantage in ASEAN import products can restrict potential benefits that it could derive from ASEAN-India FTA in Goods.

5.6 CONCLUSION

An analysis of India's competitiveness with regards to ASEAN has been presented in this chapter, based the 4 indices of RCA calculated for India's trade with ASEAN for the ten country grouping over eight years 2008 to 2017, for 37 product groups under 7 specific product categories. The "Relative Trade advantage" was observed in the case of 22 specific product groups, and these commodities constitute major export products. India could potentially trade with the ASEAN countries. The coefficient of variation was lower for these commodities, and it indicates the indices were quite stable during the 10 years.

Some product groups where a 'switch' in the opposite direction was observed, i.e., an RCD in the year 2008 but RCA in the year 2018 and constituted about 52 % of the value of the commodities in either of these years. It shows that the India's RCA has not changed much during the study period in its basic structure. The analysis presented using the B index illustrates that India is losing the comparative advantage, coinciding with the decrease in the volume of exports from India to the ASEAN countries owing to a decline concerning the fall in commodity prices against due to the global economic slowdown. The findings also suggest that India did not have comparative advantage in the short term. The values of Lafay's index present that India's need to diversify its commodity specialization pattern to match with the ASEAN counterparts. 15 product groups in which India ranks first are not listed in the import basket of the ASEAN-10. The 33 product groups where India has positive Lafay's index, but when compared with the ASEAN countries, this is negligible. Also, the lack of comparative advantage for India in the products imported by ASEAN could potentially block India to derive benefits from ASEAN-India FTA in Goods.

Although progress has been made in the last 25 years in relations between India-ASEAN, a lot can be done to further the growth in the relationship. To become a credible partner of the ASEAN by accelerating its domestic and economic connectivity across the region, and further boosting its engagement with regional institutions. India and the ASEAN countries have common goals that coincide with peaceful development of the region with prosperity and security. Tariff structures and other factors such as Distance, FTAs, common border and language are determinants of trade between India and ASEAN countries. These factors are analyzed in the next chapter by using the Augmented gravity model.

6

An Analysis of India's Trade with the ASEAN: Augmented Gravity Model Approach

Of late, international trade and manufacturing have increasingly being influenced by the growth of Asian economies, especially India and China. The global markets are being driven by the growth in the manufacturing sector in Asia, and Asia has become the provider of services and goods to the developed countries in the West. Consequently, new regional groupings and trade blocks have been formed and emerged as an effective alternative to the traditional economies. These trade blocs such as MERCOSUR, ASEAN and NAFTA have become competing entities, thus promoting regionalism in International trade. ASEAN has been growing with performing trade indicators and now targeting to merge into "Asian Economic Community" in future. Although India followed multilateralism, it has shifted gears and signed many agreements of bilateral trade with neighboring partners in trade such as Thailand, Singapore, Sri Lanka etc. In this process, India signed FTA with ASEAN grouping. This chapter uses "Augmented Gravity

Model" with Panel Data method and analyzes effect on India-ASEAN trade due to the FTA.

6.1 OBJECTIVES OF THE STUDY

1. To understand the factors that determine trade flows between ASEAN and India, using the Gravity model.
2. To analyze whether factors such as distance, population, GDP have any influence on the India-ASEAN trade.
3. To assess whether the Free Trade Agreement has any influence on the India-ASEAN bilateral trade

6.2 GRAVITY MODEL OF TRADE FOR FREE TRADE AGREEMENTS

The equation of the Gravity Model is widely used in international trade literature, considered as a very efficient empirical model in economics. The theory states that bilateral trade between any two countries is directly related to the size of the economies (GDP), and negatively related to the distance between them. While the importance of GDP is discussed well in the trade literature, the role of distance is a mystery. The Gravity Models that are used in the trade analyses are found to be very useful, and they generally use the parameters such as GDP, Population, Distance as factors that determine the flows of trade between two countries. In order to study the relevance of formation of the regional grouping, or to join an FTA, a dummy variable is inserted in the equation of gravity model, and its impact is analyzed by calculating the expected variation compared to the normal baseline trade. "The gravity model of bilateral trade, in its most basic form shows the trade between country 'i' and country 'j' is proportional to the product of GDPi and GDPj and inversely related to the distance between them. It can be expressed in the following equation form:

$$GFij=MiMj/Dij2\ i\neq j\ (1)\quad GFij=MiMj/Dij2\ i\neq j\ (1)$$

By making the log transformation Equation, 1 becomes a linear equation which can be expressed as below.

$$lnGFij=lnMi+lnMj-lnDij\ i\neq j\ (2)$$

The economic mass in equation (2) can be represented in four alternate methods namely Gross Domestic Product (GDP) of the countries, GDP and population of the countries, GDP per capita and both GDP and GDP per capita put together". (Sarath Chandran, 2018)

6.2.1. Research Methodology (Gravity Model in International Trade)

The justification for the gravity model derives from Newton's physics. Today Gravity models are generally employed to assess the influence of Regional Trade Arrangements. Another justification for the equation of gravity model can be referred to Linneman (1966) who analysed the *"export supply and the import demand in the light of a partial equilibrium model"* through Linneman approach. Few others also opined that the "partial equilibrium model is not able to explain the multiplicative form of the equation and left some of its parameters unidentified due to the exclusion of the price variable" (Bergstrand, 1985). Another method is based on Walrasian general equilibrium model, with supply and demand functions of each country included. According to this approach, supply in the country that exports and the demand in the country that imports, depend on aggregate income. Anderson's approach is based on the macro-economic variable of income, whereas Bergstrand's equation is based on microeconomic approach. Bergstrand argues that since endogenous variables are eliminated from the explanatory part of the reduced form of equation, prices and income are considered as independent variables. Thus, the author takes income and price terms as explanatory variables instead of substituting all the endogenous variables. The derived model is called a "generalized gravity equation model". Deardorff (1997) says "there is some similarity between the Heckscher-Ohlin model and Gravity Model". According to the H-O theory, capital-rich countries produce capital-intensive goods. According to Markusen (1986), affluent consumers use capital intensive goods. By extending this logic, the countries rich in capital resources will trade with similar capital endowed countries. The same is true for countries who do not have capital resources trade with similar countries with low capital resources. Linder Hypothesis (Frankel, 1997) also advocates the use of "per capita GNP" as an independent and separate variable because it denotes the status of development in the country. As the per capita GNP grows, the development also takes place, and the consumers demand more fashionable and superior products. As there is more development in the economy, there will be inventions and innovations and newer products would come into the market, and consumers demand these in other countries with similar higher per capita GNP. Advanced countries also tend to develop advanced infrastructure for transportation of goods, and the transportation convenience and distance impacts the trade between two countries. According to Bergstrand's general equilibrium approach, the size of the countries denoted by their income level, and the distance between the countries significantly impact the trade volumes between those countries.

The costs that are associated with international trade include shipping costs, time that is gone for transportation and the costs associated with unfamiliarity. "Among these costs, shipping costs are obvious" (Frankel 1997 quoted from Linnemann 1966). Most of the studies based on general equilibrium approach derived that "the population sizes of the trading countries are to have a negative and statistically significant effect on trade flows" (Linnemann 1966, Sapir 1981, Bikker 1987). There could be some exceptions to this, such as trade barriers including tariff, have a substantial adverse impact on trade volumes between the countries. Conversely, "*Preferential Trade Agreements* (PTAs)are found to be having a positive impact on trade and they are statistically significant" (Oguledo and Macphee 1994).

The basic idea to add dummy variable Free Trade Area (FTA) in the standard equation of gravity model is to capture the deviations from the normal level and course of trade as a result of FTA agreement. The dummy variable's value is taken as 1 when both the countries under the study are in the same trading or regional group and as 0 if these countries fall in different groups. The coefficient of the dummy variable, in this case, the Free Trade Area, will indicate the additional trade that is generated because of the two countries participated in the Free Trade Area. Some other factors that influence trade can be included in the basic Gravity Model. These can include factors such as cultural, geographical and historical factors.

6.2.2 The Panel Data Gravity Model

The panel data regression has a double subscript for its variables. Hence it is different from the normal time series regression or cross-section regression models. Hence,

"$y_{it} = \alpha + X'_{it}\beta + u_{it} \quad i = 1, \ldots, N; \; t = 1, \ldots T$

Where 'i'*denotes* households, individuals, firms, countries etc. and 't' is representing the time. The *i subscript*, therefore, denotes the *cross-section dimension* whereas t denotes the *time-series dimension*. α is a scalar, β is K x 1 and Xit is the ith observation on the K explanatory variables."

6.2.3 "The Fixed Effect Vector Decomposition (FEVD) Method"

"The effect of explanatory variables which are not time-dependent (*Time-Invariant Variables*), on the dependent variable cannot be calculated using the Fixed Effects model as there is no variation in the data. To address this problem, a different methodology with decomposition method is used. The Fixed Effects Vector Decomposition (FEVD) technique involves the following three steps: First, the estimation of the unit fixed effects by the baseline panel fixed effects model leaving the time-invariant but not the rarely changing right-hand side variables. Second, the regression of the fixed effects vector on the time-invariant and rarely changing explanatory variables of the original model (by OLS) to decompose the unit-specific effects into a part explained by the time-invariant variables and an unexplained part. Moreover, now the third, estimation of a pooled OLS model by including all the explanatory time-variant variables, the time-invariant variables, the rarely changing variables and the unexplained part of the fixed effects vector. This stage is required to control for the multicollinearity and to adjust the degrees of freedom in estimating the standard errors of the coefficients". (Sarath Chandran, 2018)

6.3 ANALYSIS OF THE DATA AND THE RESULTS

For the analysis, the data was taken from several sources. Data related to bilateral trade, exports, imports of countries were taken from "World Integrated Trade System (WITS)" managed by the "International Monetary Fund (IMF)", "United Nations Conference for Trade & Development (UNCTAD)" and the "World Trade Organization (WTO)". Some of the data of disaggregated trade as per HS-2 classification was taken from UN COMTRADE database of the United Nations. The data related to the country's per capita GDP, GDP and Population are taken out of "world trade indicators" of the "World Bank". Other databases used included Jon Haveman's data on the geographic distances between countries, and the common borders etc .and website of CEPII, France for the language.

The data has been taken from India and the ASEAN regional grouping for the period of 25 years from 1991 to 2016.

Analysis is carried out on balanced panel data set across different gravity variables and by using two types of "Augmented Gravity Model". Various panel estimation methods namely, (i) "Pooled OLS method (POLS)", (ii) "Maximum likelihood Estimation Method (MLE)", (iii)"Fixed Effect with Vector Decomposition (FEVD)", (iv)"Between Effect (BE)" (v) "Random Effect Method (RE)" were adapted for data analysis and deciding on reasonable model for deriving required results.

6.3.1 Specification of the Gravity Model

Two types of "Augmented Gravity Model" are employed in this chapter. The first type of model uses GDP, which is the economic factor. Few conventional gravity variables and augmented variables are also used. The total bilateral trade between country 'i' (India) and country "j" of ASEAN countries is used as a dependent variable of the model. The model employed in the study is given below:

$$\ln(TT_{ij}) = \alpha + \beta_1 \ln GDP_i + \beta_2 \ln GDP_j + \beta_3 \ln PCGDP_i + \beta_4 \ln PCGDP_j + \beta_5 \ln PCGDP_{diff} - \beta_6 \ln Distance + \beta_7 ASEAN\ member + \beta_8 Cont\ Bord + \beta_9 Com\ Lang + \beta_{10} Com\ Colony + \varepsilon_{ij}$$

Here,

Ln $(TT)_{ij}$ = Log of Total trade between country i and j for a year

Ln GDP_i = log of GDP of country i

Ln GDP_j = log of GDP of country j

Ln $PCGDP_i$ = log of per capita income of country i

Ln $PCGDP_j$ = log of per capita income of country j

Ln PCGDP diff = absolute difference in per capita of country i and j

Ln Distance = log of geographical distance between country i and j

ASEAN member = dummy representing common membership to ASEAN FTA

Cont Border = dummy if countries share common border

Com Lang = dummy if countries share common official language

Com Colony = dummy if both countries were under the same colonizer

ε_{ij} = Error term

Table 1 given below gives the calculation outcome of Augmented Gravity Model. All of the variables exhibit significant relation in explaining the bilateral trade among the countries. The variables related to the GDP of the country 'i' and the country 'j' present a positive sign and are confirming the theory, exhibiting that countries which have higher GDP have a tendency to be trading more among themselves. However, the differences in per-capita GDP of a country 'i' and the country 'j' present a negative value, and this is possibly because the GDP and per capita GDP have collinearity between them.

Referring to the augmented variables that are taken for analysis, variables like common language and the colony impact the trade positively, whereas the common border is revealing a negative influence. The co-efficient of ASEAN dummy is remarkably higher in the forecast error variance decomposition (FEVD) which is 3.5043 which is higher compared to the other estimation methods used.

Table 6.1 Results of the Augmented Gravity Model-I

Independent Variable	Dependent Variable= Total Bilateral Trade between i and j				
	Pooled OLS	MLE Method	Fixed Effect with Vector Decomposition	Between Effect Model	Random Effect Model
Ln GDPi	0.6850*** -0.0085	0.8296*** -0.0284	2.5272***	0.6841*** -0.0316	0.8421*** 0.0262
Ln GDPj	0.6772*** -0.0085	0.8116*** -0.0281	2.07***	0.6728*** -0.0206	0.8158*** 0.0254
Ln PC GDPi	0.2104*** -0.0085	0.0345 -0.032	-1.7328***	0.2032*** -0.0327	0.0442 0.0274
Ln PC GDPj	0.1595*** -0.0077	-0.0056 -0.031	-1.5607***	0.1712*** -0.0207	0.0027 0.0293
Ln PC GDPdiff	0.0723*** -0.0076	0.0016 -0.0102	-0.0107***	0.0828*** -0.0518	-0.0019 0.0101
Ln Dist	-0.8813*** -0.0249	-0.8311*** -0.0523	-0.5382***	-0.8866*** -0.0518	-0.8427*** 0.0531
ASEAN Dummy	1.3364*** -0.0505	1.6649*** -0.2129	3.5043***	1.5382*** -0.2138	1.6638*** 0.2186
Cont Border	0.0561 -0.0538	-0.1452 -0.2029	-1.3402***	0.0715 -0.1942	-0.1385 0.188
Com Language	0.3313*** -0.0182	0.3952*** -0.1048	0.8345***	0.3292*** -0.1	0.3920*** 0.1033
Colony	-0.0318 -0.0442	0.0202 -0.1542	0.4744***	-0.0328 -0.1561	0.0176 0.1604
Constant	3.1216*** -0.1411	4.4214*** -0.4287	14.2364***	3.1450*** -0.4398	4.4381*** 0.5123
Adj R Squared	0.78				12152.14 Wald Chi2(10)
F (10, 11039)	3822.03		17151.53 F (8,11038)		-8761.44 Hausman Test Chi2(10)
Breusch- Pagan/ Cook-Weisberg test Chi 2 (1)	737.68	7662.65 LR Chi2(10)		281.52 F (10,538)	43544.44 B&P LM

Note: *, **, *** shows significance at 1%, 5% and 10% respectively

Source: Authors Calculation based on data extracted

Analyzing the common border and the colony, the values are found to be not substantial in the model of Between Effect Method compared to Pooled OLS method and MLE method. Also, a careful analysis presents the Random Effect (RE) method and the method of MLE have given insignificant results of per capita GDP (i), per capita GDP (j) and the per capita GDP difference, common border and common colony (Table.6.1)

6.3.2 Results of the Augmented Gravity Model 2

The above Table. 2 presents in the chapter is the augmented gravity model 2 which replaces GDP related variables with population vaiable so that the issue arising out of the problem of endogeneity is addressed, because the same equation includes of GDP and the per capita income. Other variables which were used in Augmented model are retained in this equation.

$$\ln(TTij) = \alpha + \beta 1 \ln POPi + \beta 2 \ln POPj + \beta 3 \ln PCGDPi + \beta 4 \ln PCGDPj + \beta 5 \ln PCGDPdiff - \beta 6 \ln Distance + \beta 7 ASEANmember + \beta 8 ContBord + \beta 9 ComLang + \beta 10 ComColony + \varepsilon_{ij}$$

The model presents that all the variables in the Pooled OLS model are significant except the continuous border and the common colony. In Augmented Gravity Model-2, there is a significant improvement in the coefficients of per capita income of the country 'i' and the country 'j" over the previous model. When the MLE method includes population, Per-capita income of country 'i' and the country 'j' have become highly significant. In this model-2, the best results are presented by FEVD model. All the determinant variables in the model return higher values with a positive sign (leaving the variable continuous border) with ASEAN dummy variable getting high coefficients. The Random Effects (RE) model and the Between Effect (BE) model have given outcome that are similar compared with the results of POLS and MLE,

Table 6.2 Results of Augmented Gravity Model-2

	Pooled OLS	MLE Method	Fixed Effect with Vector Decomposition	Between Effect Model	Random Effect Model
Ln POPi	0.6750*** -0.0082	0.8356*** -0.0285	2.2273***	0.6241*** -0.0326	0.8221*** -0.0262
Ln POPj	0.6872*** -0.0085	0.8116*** -0.0281	2.07***	0.6628*** -0.0206	0.8156*** -0.0254
Ln PC GDPi	0.8893*** -0.0072	0.8651 -0.017	0.5421***	0.8833*** -0.0327	0.8762*** -0.017
Ln PC GDPj	0.8458*** -0.0077	-0.0058 -0.032	0.5607***	0.8712*** -0.0207	0.8185*** -0.0165
Ln PC GDPdiff	0.0723*** -0.0076	0.0016 -0.0102	-0.0107***	0..8328*** -0.0518	-0.8418*** 0.0531
Ln Dist	-0.8813*** -0.0249	-0.8311*** -0.0523	-0.5382***	-0.8866*** -0.0518	-0.8427*** 0.0531
ASEAN Dummy	1.4364*** -0.0505	1.6649*** -0.2129	3.5043***	1.4282*** -0.2138	1.6638*** 0.2186
Cont Border	0.0561 -0.0538	-0.1452 -0.2029	-1.3402***	0.0715 -0.1943	-0.1385 0.188
Com Language	0.3313*** -0.0182	0.3852*** -0.2048	0.8345***	0.3292*** -0.1	0.3920*** -0.1033
Colony	-0.0318 -0.0442	0.0202 -0.1542	0.4744***	0 -0.1561	0.0176 -0.1504
Constant	-6.1216*** -0.1411	-6.8894*** -0.4287	-14.7964***	-6.1545*** -0.5398	-6.8451*** -0.5123
F (10,11039)	77.02				12052.14 Wald Chi2(10)
F (10, 11039)	3822.03		17151.53 F (8,11038)		-8761.44 Hausman Test Chi2(10)
Breusch- Pagan/ Cook-Weisberg test Chi 2 (1)	737.68	7650.65 LR Chi2(10)		281.53 F (10,538)	43544.44 B&P LM TestChi2(1)

Note: *, **, *** shows significance at 1%, 5% and 10% respectively

Source: Authors Calculation based on data extract

respectively. Augmented Gravity model 1 and 2, employed for assessing the two-way trade between ASEAN and India imply a positive and significantly dummy coefficient.

Here the dummy coefficient is RTA (Regional Trade Agreement), and hence it implies that two-way trade between the two regions can be improved by the formation of an RTA. The Augmented model-2 presents a greater picture than the augmented model -1 as more positive signs are yielded, which are in accordance with the theory and addresses the endogeneity problem.

Lastly, to select among the models of "Between Effect (BE)" and the "Fixed Effects", the "Hausman model selection test" has been taken up. The value returned for the "P-value of Chi-square" is lower than 0.05 (significant value) and based on this, the "Fixed Effect model" is chosen over the "Random Effects model".

6.4 CONCLUSION

From the above analysis, it can be viewed that the values of the Pooled OLS Model resulting parameters hold the positive values and also have highly significant coefficients, but the model is unable to explain the respective attributes of the countries that could be essential determinants of bilateral trade between countries. The results of the Between Effects Model are found closer to the Pooled OLS method, and the Maximum Likelihood Estimation Method and Random Effects Method have given similar results. In the REM too, the crucial parameters taken for the study are found to be significant and showing anticipated values with a positive dummy variable ASEAN, which presented the effectiveness of the model, but there is a lack of correlation concerning the explanatory variable which presents the inefficiency of the model. A thorough comparison of the models across reveals that the augmented Gravity Model 2 is best suited to the explanation of the bilateral trade between India and ASEAN with better parameters and results that explain very well. In order to further validate, the Hausman specification test is performed and it presented a positive note. The ASEAN dummy results return with the highest coefficient. The chapter explains the positive influence of the Regional Trade Agreement on trade between India and the ASEAN countries. Also, it is possible for ASEAN countries could benefit more in the short-term because the initial levels of tariff are lower in ASEAN when compared to that of India. Free Trade Agreement (FTA) should be extended to include service and investments, beyond trade in goods, to realize the full potentiality in trade with ASEAN countries,

7

An Analysis of Intra-Industry Trade and Tariff Structures of India and the ASEAN Nations

As a part of liberalization policy, India expanded its capacity by unveiling its 'Look East Policy' during the early 1990s. Since then, it has been put at the priority level in International affairs policy of India. India had a historical link with Southeast Asia as a region with which it could share a safe, secure and war free relationship. To fulfil the purpose, India showed interest in ASEAN region. India started its association with ASEAN by becoming a sectoral dialogue partner initially and a full dialogue partner in the year 1995. The volume of trade between India and ASEAN gradually has been rising. The relationship has been evolved very noticeable over the years. Even more than commercial engagements, a comprehensive and balanced partnership is being shared between ASEAN and India, including cultural exchanges, emotional linkages, people to people and all around and wide-ranging relationship. ASEAN was also speedily liberalizing its market opportunities. It also observed the need to develop courtship with India so that both could work together to address the opportunities and challenges of globalization and liberalization. The bilateral *Free Trade*

Agreements (FTA) signed from time to time, and other activities intensified ASEAN's economic relations with India and these FTAs are regarded as part of India's 'Look East Policy'. ASEAN too understands the necessity to get closer to India in order to grow a more balanced relationship with all the major Asian economies.

India and ASEAN have progressed their relationship further over time. They both realized the favourable circumstances to increase business relations between them and started negotiating on a framework agreement to establish "ASEAN-India Free Trade Area". During the second "India-ASEAN summit" in 2003, the "ASEAN-India Framework Agreement on Comprehensive Economic Co-operation" (asean.org) was signed. This agreement eventually became base for constituting an "India-ASEAN Regional Trade and Investment Area", that comprises of FTAs goods as well as investments and services. India and ASEAN signed the "ASEAN-India Trade -in- Goods Agreement" in Thailand on August 13, 2009, which got implemented form January 1, 2010. By signing this agreement, India and ASEAN have paved way for establishing one among the largest free trade regions of the world. The tariff structures need to be gradually decreased and eliminated between the two, to reap the fullest potential of the FTA agreement. A tariff is a vital and most influencing factor in the trading regime of the countries. The current Chapter would focus on the *"Intra-Industry Trade"* of India and the ASEAN countries. As with growing globalization and technological advancement, the commodity patterns and product categories have been on the rise giving rise to the more and more intra trade.

The Chapter has five sections. Section-I presents the objectives of the Chapter. Section-II gives the methodology adopted in the Chapter, Section-III presents the *"Intra industry trade index"* of India and the ASEAN. The Fourth

Section gives a glance on the Tariff structures between India and the ASEAN and analysis on the trade agreements between India and the ASEAN. V Section gives the significant findings of the Chapter, and the last section-VI summarises the conclusion.

7.1. OBJECTIVES OF THE STUDY

- To analyze the Intra industry trade of India and the ASEAN nations.
- To present an analytical view about FTA between India and the ASEAN nations.

7.2 METHODOLOGY

A combination of analytical and descriptive methods has been used in this Chapter. To Calculate the "Intra-Industry Trade", the "Grubel and Lloyd index" has been adopted.

The **Grubel–Lloyd index** (GL Index) "measures *Intra-Industry Trade* of a particular product. The GL Index was propounded by *Herb Grubel* and *Peter Lloyd* in 1971.

$$GL_i = \frac{(X_i + M_i) - |X_i - M_i|}{X_i + M_i} = 1 - \frac{|X_i - M_i|}{X_i + M_i} \quad ; 0 \leq GL_i \leq 1$$

where X_i = the export, M_i =import of good *i*."

(Grubel, Herb; Llyod, Peter 1971)

In case GL_i is 1, the entire trade becomes *"Intra-Industry Trade"*, and zero *"Inter-Industry Trade"*. In such a case, the subject country exports as well as imports the same volume of good *i*. If GL_i = 0, it means that the *"Inter-Industry Trade"* prevails and zero *"Intra-Industry Trade"*, where the subject country imports or exports the product 'i' but not both.

7.3 AN ANALYSIS OF INTRA INDUSTRY TRADE INDEX OF INDIA AND ASEAN NATIONS

In the modern globalized world, international trade is increasingly becoming Intra Industry Trade, when commodities belonging to the same product group are increasingly being traded, intra-industry trade has been accelerating. The Intra Industry Trade of India and the ASEAN nations for the period 2012-2017 is calculated following the Gruel-Lloyd (G-L) Index for India and the ASEAN nations, and the average is taken into account for analyzing the *Intra-Industry Trade* of the nations for 57 commodity category under 10 categories as per the Lemer's Aggregation Scheme.

As the country's economy starts growing value of "Intra Industry Trade" increases. Large part of the trade in the world is the "Intra-Industry Trade" in many advanced economies. Table. 7.1 provides the values of "Intra-Industry trade" (IIT) of India and the ASEAN economies. The values of "G-L index of intra-industry trade" is higher for ASEAN economies, and it proves they are more integrated into the world economy. Higher values of IIT index provide greater integration with the global economy and openness in economies. The IIT index for India presents that more than 10 commodities present a value which is less than 0.0, presenting no intra trade in these commodity categories like Petroleum, crude fertilizers, natural gas, fertilizers and plates etc, more than 30 commodities present an IIT value which is more than 0.50 presenting a significant number of these commodities are exported and imported, almost all the commodities under tropical agriculture, animal product group, cereals, labour intensive category and capital intensive manufactures, machinery have presented this for India. Overall the increasing amount of Intra-trade of the ASEAN nations presents the untapped potential for India's trade with ASEAN.

Table 7.1 Intra Industry Trade (2012-2017 Average)

	India	Brunei	Cambodia	Indonesia	Laos	Malaysia	Myanmar	Phillippines	Singapore	Thailand	Vietnam
Petroleum											
Petroleum oils, oils from bitumin. materials, crude	0	0	0.02	0.42	0	0.77	0	0.19	0.04	0.05	0.14
Raw Materials											
Crude fertilizers (excluding those of division 56)	0.01	0.14	0.03	0.38	0.05	0.25	0.03	0.23	0.44	0.37	0.87
Other crude minerals	0.83	0.06	0	0.79	0.15	0.44	0.14	0.11	0.81	0.83	0.43
Ores and concentrates of base metals, n.e.s.	0.45	*	0.06	0.78	0.03	0.89	0.36	0.14	0.63	0.08	0.41
Coke & semi-cokes of coal, lign., peat; retort carbon	0.04	*	*	*	0.03	0.03	*	0	0.35	0.14	0.4
Natural gas, whether or not liquefied	0.01	0	0	0.26		0.13	0	0.23	0.07	0.04	0.33
Non-ferrous base metal waste and scrap, n.e.s.	0.02	0.01	0.02	0.77	0.86	0.56	0.51	0.2	0.42	0.04	0.68
Forest products											
Wood manufacture, n.e.s.	0.68	0.26	0.4	0.25	0.6	0.28	0.54	0.1	0.23	0.53	0.13
Paper and paperboard	0.28	0.04	0	0.6	0	0.4	0.01	0.21	0.86	0.86	0.2
Cork manufactures	0.05	0.25	0.64	0.68	0.14	0.83	0.17	0.53	0.73	0.12	0.59
Pulp and wastepaper	0.28	0.01	0.02	0.77	0.86	0.56	0.51	0.2	1	0.04	0.68

Tropical Agriculture											
Fruits and nuts (excluding oil nuts), fresh or dried	0.59	0.01	0.47	0.83	0.34	0.38	0.38	0.3	0.31	0.3	0.57
Oil seeds & oleaginous fruits (incl. flour, n.e.s.)	0.77	0.13	0.32	0.82	0.06	0.59	0.01	0.01	0.43	0.38	0.57
Fixed vegetable fats & oils, crude, refined, fract.	0.11	0	0	0.44	0.01	0.89	0.04	0.25	0.25	0.56	0.82
Sugar, molasses and honey	0.7	0.01	0.21	0.42	0.82	0.29	0.82	0.61	0.46	0.18	0.73
Coffee and coffee substitutes	0.54	0.02	0	0.42	0.38	0.85	0.1	0.01	0.85	0.74	0.04
Chocolate, food preparations with cocoa, n.e.s.	0.68	0.01	0.02	0.75	0.01	0.92	0.03	0.25	0.66	0.56	0.62
Non-alcoholic beverages, n.e.s.	0.76	0	0.04	0.36	0.43	0.83	0.62	0.13	0.59	0.39	0.63
Animal products											
Animals oils and fats	0.55	0.19	0.01	0.75	0.07	0.28	0.13	0.06	0.2	0.41	0.72
Animal or veg. oils & fats, processed, n.e.s.; mixt.	0.03	0	0.04	0.36	0.01	0.29	0.07	0.5	0.37	0.69	0.57
Live animals other than animals of division 03	0.77	0.01	0.41	0.47	0.13	0.62	0.45	0.54	0.04	0.75	0.23
Meat of bovine animals, fresh, chilled or frozen	0.5	0	0.01	0.5	0.1	0.08	0.14	0	0.15	0.17	0.02
Hides and skins (except furskins), raw	0.03	0.47	0.3	0.36	0.44	0.79	0.28	0.47	0.39	0.07	0.12
Crude animal materials, n.e.s.	0.73	0.06	0	0.36	0.59	0.05	0.14	0.11	0.81	0.83	0.43
Fish, fresh (live or dead), chilled or frozen	0.5	0.02	0.01	0.37	0.01	0.92	0.37	0.04	0.33	0	0.02

	India	Brunei	Cambodia	Indonesia	Laos	Malaysia	Myanmar	Phillippines	Singapore	Thailand	Vietnam
Cereals											
Cereals, unmilled (excluding wheat, rice, barley, maize)	0.56	0.01	0.76	0.34	0.21	0.01	0.45	0	0.01	0.88	0
Feeding stuff for animals (no unmilled cereals)	0.58	0.01	0.25	0.58	0.02	0.61	0.04	0.18	0.6	0.91	0.26
Tobacco, manufactured	0.53	0.12	0.09	0.33	0.68	0.82	0.59	0.36	0.86	0.84	0.23
Wool and other animal hair (incl. wool tops)	0.55	0.31	0.09	0.36	0.28	0.46	0.02	0.16	0.58	0.75	0.2
Worn clothing and other worn textile articles	0.56	-	-	0.88	-	-	-	0	0.68	-	-
Milk, cream and milk products (excluding butter, cheese)	0.62	0.02	0	0.44	0.08	0.57	0.01	0.15	0.56	0.54	0.32
Labour intensive manufactures											
Mineral manufactures, n.e.s.	0.61	0.11	0.03	0.81	0.07	0.65	0.01	0.67	0.72	0.36	0.97
Furniture & parts	0.94	0.03	0.77	0.62	0.61	0.39	0.29	0.86	0.22	0.36	0.08
Travel goods, handbags & similar containers	0.6	0.12	0.39	0.88	-	0.26	0.43	0.5	0.54	0.5	-
Articles of apparel, clothing access., excluding textile	0.56	-	-	-	0.75	-	-	-	0.68	-	0.06
Footwear	0.57	0.05	0.2	0.37	0.46	0.55	0.59	0.34	0.53	0.48	0.09
Gold, non-monetary (excluding gold ores and concentrates)	0.34	0.06	0	0.4	0.15	0.44	0.14	0.11	0.93	0.83	0.41
Miscellaneous manufactured articles, n.e.s.	0.19	0.01	0.4	0.81	0.4	0.65	0	0.67	0	0.35	0.19

Capital Intensive Manufactures											
Leather	0.68	0.68	0.03	0.35	0.4	0.25	0.08	0.06	0.64	0.26	0.41
Rubber tyres, tyre treads or flaps & inner tubes	0.25	0	0.6	0.71	0.18	0.22	0.07	0.42	0.87	0.01	0.69
Textile yarn	0.55	0.06	0	0.61	0.03	0.49	0	0.25	0.56	0.27	0.66
Wire of iron or steel	0.6		0	0.41	.	0.89	0.22	0.43	0	0.26	0.48
Manufactures of base metal, n.e.s.	0.13	0.12	0.02	0.38	0.52	0.58	0.03	0.12	0.01	0.25	0
Sanitary, plumbing, heating fixtures, fittings, n.e.s.	0.86	0.09	0	0.91	0.01	0.83	0.03	0.19	0.15	0.39	0.32
Articles of apparel, of textile fabrics, n.e.s.	0.63	0.01	0.68	0.88	0.82	0.73	0.48	0.77	0.68	0.39	0.93
Machinery											
Office machines	0.13	0.04	0.03	0.48	0.02	0.56	0	0.49	0.93	0.07	0.18
Household type equipment, electrical or not, n.e.s.	0.1	0.14	0.05	0.92	0.02	0.58	0.04	0.09	0.04	0.25	0.31
Motor vehicles for the transport of persons	0.6	0.01	0.01	0.46	0.02	0.04	0.01	0	0.38	0.45	0.03
Electrical machinery & apparatus, n.e.s.	0.38	0.36	0.04	0.94	0.06	0.88	0.02	0.58	0.88	0.36	0.6

Chemicals											
Inorganic chemical elements, oxides & halogen salts	0.26	0.01	0.01	0.56	0.01	0.61	0.01	0.18	0.72	0.2	0.03
Dyeing & tanning extracts, synth. tanning materials	0.61	0.43	0	0.57		0.8	0.39	0.03	0.83	0.63	0.01
Medicinal and pharmaceutical products, excluding 542	0.94	0.05	0.1	0.42	0.02	0.58	0	0.06	0.53	0.75	0.05
Fertilizers (other than those of group 272)	0.01	0.12	0	0.55	0.77	0.58	0	0.15	0.34	0.39	0.37
Explosives and pyrotechnic products	0.78	0.09	0	0.34	0.06	0.73	0	0.64	0.74	0.48	0.48
Miscellaneous chemical products, n.e.s.	0.51	0.33	0	0.34	0.06	0.93	0	0.57	0.91	0.9	0.52
Essential oils, perfume & flavor materials	0.6	0.01	0.04	0.35	0.21	0.25	0.01	0.14	0.34	0.53	0.08
Plates, sheets, films, foil & strip, of plastics	0.07	0.06	0.41	0.54	0.18	0.22	0.07	0.47	0.53	0.44	0.69
Arms & ammunition	0.73		0.1	0.31	0.09	0.3	0.02	0.67	0.52	0.38	-

Source: Author's Calculation based on data extracted from unctad.org

Brunei has displayed an IIT index where IIT index close to zero for all the commodities except for 11 commodities, the highest IIT index for Brunei is displayed by Leather (0.682). Cambodia too being a smaller economy except for 15 product categories other 42 product categories no significant value of Intra trade is registered. Indonesia is one economy where all the products have registered with significant IIT value indices, and 28 commodities have IIT value more than 0.50 presenting growing intra trade for these product categories like ores & concentrates, crude minerals, animal oils & fats, cereals, worn clothing, sanitary, plumbing, articles of apparels and chemicals. Laos have presented IIT value for nonferrous base metal (0.856) and rest 26 commodities found to have insignificant IIT value which is 0.0. Malaysia one of the economically progressive country with the highest number of ports in Asia presented insignificant values of IIT for only four commodities, and all the other product groups analyzed presented significant IIT values and growing dynamism in the Intra Trade. In the case of Myanmar, the values present no IIT trade with respect to commodity groups of Chemicals, Machinery and Capital-Intensive Manufactures. Philippines displayed higher IIT values for Travel goods and furniture and only 13 commodity categories presented low IIT values. Singapore is transit nations primarily know for entrepot and reexport trade; therefore, high and the IIT values represent significant Intra trade analyzed, except for commodities of natural resources viz. Natural gas, live animals, cereals unmilled, miscellaneous manufactured articles, wires of iron and manufactured of base metal due to lack of vegetation. Thailand is one economy where insignificant trade values are registered for 9 commodities and 14 commodities for Vietnam has registered insignificant Intra- Industry Trade values. The FTA between both countries provides immense scope to tap the untapped trade potential between the groups.

7.4 ASEAN INDIA-FREE TRADE AGREEMENT-AN ANALYSIS

"Look East Policy" of India is mainly directed to develop relations with ASEAN countries both for trade and social aspects. Indian Government has placed further emphasis on this policy and re-christened as "Act East Policy". India became sectoral dialogue partner to ASEAN initially in 1992 and later became full dialogue partner in 1995. India has proceeded with a strategic partnership with ASEAN then onwards. The partnership over the years has seen expansion in trade and intensification of economic relations between two regions and the partnership reached a milestone of 25 years in 2017.

India and ASEAN together present one of the biggest economic blocs, having a population of 180 crores which is a fourth of world population and a total GDP of US$3.8 trillion. They have been establishing cooperation in various fields and implementing a different kind of projects in "agriculture, space, science and technology, environment and climate change, human resource development, capacity building, new and renewable energy, tourism, people-to-people contacts, and connectivity" (Exim Bank, 2018). As on date, projects worth 48 million US dollars were considered, and these are under implementation. Some of the projects were enumerated below.

- "Space Project" to establish a station for "tracking, data reception/data processing in Ho Chi Minh City, Vietnam;"
- Project to upgrade "telemetry tracking and command station in Biak, Indonesia";
- Project to set up "'centres of excellence in software development & training in 'CLMV' countries";
- Project to set up e-Network for the facilitation of telemedicine and tele-education in CLMV countries. (Exim Bank, 2018)

"The ASEAN - India Framework Agreement on Comprehensive Economic Cooperation" (CECA) has been signed in October 2003, to institutionalize a basis for business engagements in the next years. This agreement has led to signing the following agreements between India and ASEAN countries, which together called "ASEAN-India Free Trade Area (AIFTA)"

- Trade-in Goods Agreement
- Trade-in Services and Investment Agreement

The above two agreements are the basis of "ASEAN-India Free Trade Area" (AIFTA)". Both the regions have signed "The ASEAN-India Trade in Goods Agreement" after deliberations for six years in 2009, and it got implemented from January 1, 2010. They also signed "The ASEAN-India Agreement on Investment and Trade in Services" in November 2014, that got implemented from July 1, 2015.

7.4.1. Trade-in Goods Agreement

"The ASEAN-India Agreement on Trade in Goods" has come into force on different dates with different groups of ASEAN member states. "Malaysia, Singapore, Thailand, Vietnam, Myanmar, Indonesia, Brunei" joined the agreement on different dates from January to November 2010, followed by "Lao PDR, Philippines, Cambodia" during 2011. Similarly, the timelines for implementation of tariff reductions/elimination also have been drawn. For commodities under "normal track 1 and 2, sensitive track, special products and highly sensitive track", these tariff changes will be implemented for five countries "Singapore, Thailand, Indonesia, Malaysia, Vietnam" in 2019, followed by the Philippines in 2022, and for CLMV countries in 2024. The concessions in the tariff are sought to be implemented by either eliminating the tariff or reducing the tariff rates. **Table 7.2** gives the details of different commodity categories and the agreed structure of tariff elimination or reduction with respect to those commodities.

The agreement paves the way for the elimination of tariffs on 80% of the tariff lines over a while, and about 75% of total trade will be covered under the agreement when it is implemented fully.

India exercised exclusion of 489 HS6 Digit level tariff lines from tariff concession list and 590 tariff lines from tariff elimination list because these represent sensitive products in *"agriculture, textiles, auto, chemicals, petrochemicals, crude and refined palm oil, coffee, tea, pepper"*. (asean.org) ASEAN also exercised exclusion for each of its member state from a list of products proposed for concession or elimination of tariffs.

7.4.2 Benefits to Indian exporters under AIFTA:

- Indian products will have preferential tariff access throughout ASEAN 10 member countries.
- The elimination of tariffs of importing countries should result from a reduction in the price of products throughout ASEAN.
- Strengthen industry to face increased competition
- Help Indian products to get access into ASEAN region that can give substantial advantages.
- ASEAN consumers can get products at lower prices because the raw materials are imported by local producers at lower tariffs.
- Some of the ASEAN's processing factories can take advantage of low priced raw materials from India due to the tariff elimination, and reduce their cost of production

Table 7.2: ASEAN India Tariff Reduction/Elimination Framework

Category	Brunei, Indonesia, Malaysia, Singapore, Thailand & India	India and Philippines	Cambodia, Lao PDR, Myanmar, Vietnam (CLMV) & India
Normal Track 1	Most Favored Nation(MFN) tariff rates to be reduced to 0% by 2013	MFN tariff rates to be reduced to 0% by 2018	MFN tariff rates to be reduced to 0% for India by 2013 and 0% for CLMV by 2018
Normal Track 2	MFN tariff rates to be reduced to 0% by 2016	MFN tariff rates to be reduced to 0% by 2019	MFN tariff rates to be reduced to 0% for India by 2016 and 0% for CLMV by 2021
Sensitive Track	i. MFN tariff rates to be reduced to 5% by 2016 ii. Other than 50 tariffs lines, MFN rates to be reduced to 4.5% upon entry into force of the Agreement. Preferential Tariffs rates to be reduced to 4% by 2016.	i. MFN tariff rates to be reduced to 5% by 2019 ii. Other than 50 tariffs lines, MFN rates to be reduced to 4.5% upon entry into force of the Agreement. Preferential Tariffs rates to be reduced to 4% by 2019.	i. MFN tariff rates to be reduced to 5% by 2016 for India and for CLMV by 2021 ii. Other than 50 tariff lines, MFN rates to be reduced to 4.5% by 5 years for CLMV. Preferential Tariffs rates to be reduced to 4% by 2021.

Category	Brunei, Indonesia, Malaysia, Singapore, Thailand & India	India and Philippines	Cambodia, Lao PDR, Myanmar, Vietnam (CLMV) & India
	iii. Applied MFN tariff rates on 4 per cent of the tariff lines placed in the Sensitive Track (as will be identified by each Party) will be eliminated by 2019	iii. Applied MFN tariff rates on 4 per cent of the tariff lines placed in the Sensitive Track (as will be identified by each Party) will be eliminated by 2022	iii. Applied MFN tariff rates on 4 per cent of the tariff lines placed in the Sensitive Track (as will be identified by each Party) will be eliminated by 2024
Special Product* (Applicable for India)	MFN tariff rate to be reduced to 37.5% for crude oil, 50% for pepper, 45% for palm oil, coffee and black tea by 2019	MFN tariff rate to be reduced to 37.5% for crude oil, 50% for pepper, 45% for palm oil, coffee and black tea by 2019	MFN tariff rate to be reduced to 37.5% for crude oil, 50% for pepper, 45% for palm oil, coffee and black tea by 2019
Highly Sensitive Track (Not applicable for Brunei, Lao, Myanmar & Singapore)	MFN tariff rates to be reduced to 50% (Category 1), 50% (Category 2) and 25% (Category 3) by 2019	MFN tariff rates to be reduced to 50% (Category 1), 50% (Category 2) and 25% (Category 3) by 2022	MFN tariff rates to be reduced to 50% (Category 1), 50% (Category 2) and 25% (Category 3) by 2024
Exclusion List	Exclusion Lists shall be subject to an annual tariff review with a view to improving market access	Exclusion Lists shall be subject to an annual tariff review with a view to improving market access	Exclusion Lists shall be subject to an annual tariff review with a view to improving market access

* India's Schedule of Tariff Commitments consists of 40 items placed under Special Products falling under India's *"Highly Sensitive List"* which belong *"Crude Palm Oil (CPO), Refined Palm Oil (RPO), coffee, pepper and tea"*

Source: "ASEAN – India Trade Goods Agreement", Ministry of Commerce and Industry, Government of India.

- ASEAN member state economies can become a single market that could make it a strong economy with a large population.
- The exports and investment segments achieve greater potentiality in the extended period.
- India's export complementarities are higher with the ASEAN countries compared to other regions.

7.4.3 "ASEAN – India Agreement on Trade in Services and Investment"

"The ASEAN-India Trade in Services and Investment Agreement" (asean.org) has come in to force in 2015. The Service Agreement includes some of the articles such as "transparency, domestic regulations, recognition, market access, and national treatment, increasing participation of developing countries, the joint committee on services, review, dispute settlement and denial of benefits" (asean.org). This agreement mainly centres on the security of investments to make sure that investors are given fair and equal treatment, and also non-discriminating treatment in expropriation or nationalization, and fair compensation.

7.4.4. Advantage of FTA in services and investment

- It facilitates people movement and flow of investments between India and ASEAN
- Assists to reduce the deficit in the trade of India with ASEAN
- It has the potential to boost Indian – ASEAN trade to USD 100 billion.
- It facilitates review and settlements of disputes to sort out issues between partners.
- The FTA has an annexure that provides the flexibility of movement of Indian service

professionals such as business executives, contract service providers and other specialists, in ASEAN countries.

- It has a fundamental role in progressing towards "Regional Comprehensive Economic Partnership" (RCEP) agreement.

7.4.5. List of other agreements between India and ASEAN

- Action plan to carry out "ASEAN-INDIA Partnership for Peace, Progress and Shared Prosperity" (2016- 2020)
- The mechanism to include in the "Treaty of Amity and Cooperation in Southeast Asia by India."
- "ASEAN - India Joint Declaration for Cooperation to Combat International Terrorism", Bali, Indonesia, October 2003.

After India-ASEAN CECA came into existence, the overall trade between India and ASEAN has increased to 68.6 billion US dollars from 52.6 billion between 2010 and 2017. However, India's exports to ASEAN declined from 37.89 billion US dollars to 29 billion from 2013 to 2017. The same trend followed in India's imports from ASEAN as well, in the same period, as they reduced from USD 42.31 billion to 38.22 billion. The following segment presents an analysis of pre-AIFTA and post-AIFTA trading scenario.

7.4.6 Growth of Trade during the Pre-AIFTA Agreement

Trade relations between Indi and ASEAN have shifted from pre-AIFTA to post AIFTA period. Exports of India to ASEAN during Pre-AIFTA were growing at a CAGR of 23.39% whereas the imports have grown at a CAGR of 23.71% between 2003-09. At the same time, the trade deficit of India also has growth by 24.69% from 1.62 billion US dollars to 6.07 billion.

Table 7.3 India – ASEAN trade in the Pre-AIFTA (USD Billion)

Year	India's Exports to ASEAN	India's Imports from ASEAN	India's Trade Deficit/Surplus
2003	5.07	6.69	-1.62
2004	7.55	8.55	-1
2005	10.29	10.63	-0.35
2006	12.37	16.3	-3.93
2007	13.82	21.03	-7.21
2008	19.43	26.7	-7.26
2009	17.9	23.97	-6.07
CAGR (%)	**23.39%**	**23.71%**	**24.69%**

Source: Author's calculation from data extracted dots.org

Table 7.4 India – ASEAN trade in the Post -AIFTA (USD Billion)

Year	India's Export to ASEAN	India's Imports from ASEAN	India's Trade Deficit/Surplus
2010	22.96	29.64	-6.68
2011	34.5	40.33	-5.83
2012	32.3	42.74	-10.44
2013	37.89	42.31	-4.42
2014	31.29	44.46	-13.16
2015	26.43	41.52	-15.09
2016	26.38	38.22	-11.84
2017	30.96	40.61	-9.65
2018	34.2	47.15	-12.95
CAGR (%)	5.10%	5.97%	8.62%

Source: Author's calculation from data extracted dots.org

During the post-AIFTA regime (2010 -2018), India's export growth to ASEAN stood at a CAGR of 5.10% compared to the import growth of CAGR 5.97 % during 2010-18. Besides, the trade deficit grew at a CAGR of 18.62 % during 2010-18. The AIFTA may have decelerated the pace of growth in trade between India and ASEAN, as evident from the table below. This calls for diversification in the export basket of India. The trade gap between ASEAN and India has expanded at a greater extent over the years. The primary reason could be the trade design between India and the ASEAN. The trade complementarities are higher for ASEAN with India, which shows that the export pattern of ASEAN is more aligned to import pattern of India. Besides, the drop in tariffs has also played a catalyst. However, the extent of change has been limited.

7.5 MAJOR FINDINGS

- The *Intra Industry Trade* values of India and ASEAN nations reveal a growing amount of intra industry trade which gives the immense potential for bilateral trade between the two.
- Trade relations of India with ASEAN have significantly shifted from the Pre-AIFTA period to Post AIFTA period
- India's trade with ASEAN during the pre-AIFTA has been more than the post-AIFTA
- The reason for such a shift could be the trade design between India and the ASEAN.
- To avail the full potential of AIFTA, the agreement has to be implemented in full spirit, and there should be a greater diversification in the export basket of India.

7.6 CONCLUSION

It has taken about 10 years to establish partnership and cordial relations between India and ASEAN. India has been actively engaged with ASEAN and participated in various forums including "ASEAN Regional Forum" (ARF), the "Post Ministerial Conferences" (PMCs), and "Treaty of Amity and Cooperation in South Asia" (TAC). Recognizing the possible benefits from increased ties and cooperation in trade, both parties signed a framework agreement that could clear the path for instituting an "India-ASEAN Free Trade Area". This led to the signing of the landmark "India-ASEAN Framework Agreement for Comprehensive Economic Cooperation" in 2003 which lead to subsequent FTAs in goods, services and investments which became fully operational since 2016. The India-ASEAN FTA is essential as it was the first *Multilateral FTA* negotiated by India. The following last Chapter presents with the major findings of the research work on this topic and the conclusions.

8

Summary and Conclusions

India and South-East Asia are parts of the same geopolitical and civilizational space. History tells us that whenever cooperation has existed, both regions have prospered in peace and stability. The French author Coedes in his famous book "The Indianized States of South-East Asia" (G. Coedes, 1975) speaks of the historical imperative of cooperation and our shared destinies and inheritance. Both regions have a lot to offer and share. Hence, the study attempts to evaluate India-ASEAN trade relations.

Over the past decade, the bilateral trade between India and ASEAN has seen some growth but India's trade with ASEAN is yet to become significant. There exists an untapped potential to increase the trade between India and ASEAN considering the journey that has taken place so far. Also, going by the experience of other trade blocks that have seen significant growth, India and ASEAN can improve their bilateral trade by reducing the barriers to trade.

Tariff rates are crucial in defining the extent of trade between countries or regions. India's tariff structures have still higher rates compared to International standards. Through persistent endeavours, attempts were made to reduce tariff rates since 1995, yet there is scope to decrease the rates further through bilateral agreements. The ASEAN-

India FTA has to be implemented in full spirits. Given this, the present study focuses on the following objectives.

8.1 OBJECTIVES OF THE STUDY

- To study the bilateral trade pattern between India and the ASEAN regional group under the study period 2000 to 2017.
- To assess the trade intensities between India and ASEAN countries during the period.
- To analyze the commodity trade pattern between India and the ASEAN region and identify the commodities with the potentiality to increase the trade-in future.
- To analyze the extent of "Intra-Industry Trade" for the various commodity groups taken for the study of India and the ASEAN group and identify the direction of the trade pattern of these commodities.
- To identify the factors affecting the trade between India and the ASEAN regional group.
- To identify the areas where opportunities for trade exist between India and ASEAN, analyze prospects in future.

8.2 FINDINGS OF THE STUDY

The outline of the main findings of the study is presented below.

1. The analysis reveals that the international trade of India (imports as well as exports) is still meagre in the world trade, in comparison with its neighbours in South East Asia. Despite having a lower share in world trade, India has increased its annual average growth in both imports and exports since 2000.

2. Since 1997 relations between India and ASEAN have started developing, and India initiated the Look East Policy strategy, which later became Act East Policy. In this backdrop, the trade intensity of India with ASEAN in both exports and imports have started rising. Especially the countries of Vietnam, Myanmar, Brunei has been rising along with the other prominent trade partners of India viz. Singapore, Indonesia, Malaysia and Thailand.
3. Trade openness plays a prominent role in increasing trade volumes. Trade Openness Index of India with the ASEAN nations has been low compared with the ASEAN countries.
4. The trade share of ASEAN countries when compared with India, USA and China, presents a growing share of trade volumes with China replacing the USA. The trade share of India remains low, but on an increasing trajectory.
5. The "Export Intensity Index (XII)" and "Import Intensity Index (MII)" values present a gradually increasing trend, especially after signing the Free Trade Agreement between both the economies in 2010.
6. The Modified Trade Intensity values with respect to India with the ASEAN countries remained almost the same till the year 2009, but owing to the post-crisis strategies adopted by countries and India's new Foreign trade policies accelerating and diversifying the trade with respect of the world, there was a gradual rise exhibiting an improvement in the volume of trade of India with other countries. The CLMV strategy followed by India regarding Cambodia, Laos, Myanmar and Vietnam played a prominent role in intensifying the trade with these countries which could be observed in the

increasing intensity of trade values with these countries.

- The "Relative Trade advantage (RTA)" is observed with respect to 22 product categories with RTA>1. These commodities constitute potentially major products for India to export to ASEAN countries.
- India is losing the comparative advantage, as illustrated by B index, coinciding with the decrease in the volume of India's exports to the ASEAN countries owing to a decline concerning the fall in commodity prices against due to the global economic slowdown.
- 23 products have shown a negative LFI index where India does not have a comparative advantage, and it shows a lack of specialization.
- For the remaining 33 products, India has maintained a comparative advantage, as shown by a positive value of the LFI. However, these products are not occupying a significant share in the ASEAN imports basket.
- The findings also suggest that India did not possess a comparative advantage in the short term.
- India should transform its commodity specialization pattern to match with the ASEAN counterparts.
- Also, India's lack of comparative advantage in ASEAN import products can restrict possible gain that it could derive from ASEAN-India FTA in Goods.

7. The chapter on gravity trade strongly explains how the trade can be potentially improved between India and the ASEAN member states by entering into Regional Trading Agreement.

8. ASEAN member-states would benefit from the FTA in the short term because the tariff levels are higher in India initially.
9. For India, to realize the full potential in trade with ASEAN grouping a Free Trade Agreement (FTA) should be implemented apart from trade in goods to bring in the investment and services too.
10. The "Intra Industry Trade" values of India and ASEAN nations reveal a growing amount of intra industry trade which gives the immense potential for bilateral trade between the two.
11. India's trade with ASEAN during the pre-AIFTA has been more than the post-AIFTA. The primary reason could be the design of trade between the two regions.
12. ASEAN-India FTA holds immense opportunities for India. However, gains in trade can be considerable only if Intra-Industry trade is developed and supply chains are integrated.
13. We have proposed the following Hypotheses
    a. Ho (null): India's trade share with the ASEAN group has continuously been on the rise, and this has gained momentum during the last decade.

       H1(Alternative): India's trade share with the ASEAN group has not been on the rise during the last decade.
    b. Ho(null): There is a difference in the composition of trade between India and the ASEAN during the study period

       H1(Alternative): There is no difference in the composition of trade between India and the ASEAN during the study period.

c. Ho(null): There is a change in the pattern of commodity trade between India and the ASEAN.

   H1(Alternative): There is no change in the pattern of commodity trade between India and the ASEAN.

d. Ho(null): There is an immense scope and prospects for future trade between India and the ASEAN

   H1(Alternative): There is no scope and prospects for future trade between India and the ASEAN

Based on the analyses done in various chapters, and findings of the study, all the above null hypotheses have been accepted and alternative hypotheses rejected.

8.3. PROSPECTS OF INDIA-ASEAN RELATIONSHIP

This section focuses on the Prospects of the India and ASEAN relationship in the near future. For improving the flows of trade and investments, India and ASEAN have made agreements to develop transportation and infrastructure. Some areas have been identified to focus on the future, and these include collaboration in IT, Human Resource Development, Transport and Infrastructure, SMEs, Shipping, arresting trans-national crime, interactions between people. Also, to be focused are areas where advanced technology is used such as material science, space research, biotechnology, food security etc.

India also has come forward to help the region along the Mekong in various sectors such as water resource development, oceanography, environment protection, soil erosion, fisheries, roads, railways, agriculture etc.

Hence to accelerate the momentum of India-ASEAN trade and to push it into a higher growth trajectory, both the nations will have to put in their best efforts for exploiting the potential fully. To take advantage of the synergies, the partners have to develop new linkages and thereby create multiplier effects to achieve many-fold expansion in two-way trade flow in the coming years.

The major obstacles that lead to India's meagre performance in exports to the ASEAN market include fierce competition from China and the enforcement of non-tariff barriers. The non-tariff barriers (NTMs) in the ASEAN countries have slowed down the integration of products from India into ASEAN. As per the WTO data, the NTMs accounted for a rise of 1634 from the year 2000 to 5,975 during the period 2015.

China is among the biggest exporters to ASEAN countries in a large number of products. India's engagement with ASEAN has been obstructed by the increased competition from China for electrical equipment, mechanical appliances, plastics, iron and steel and organic chemicals among the others. To move forward, in order to increase India's presence in the ASEAN market, India should fully utilize the potential of the ASEAN Economic Community (AEC). In addition to counter the onslaught of trade deficit that India had incurred over the years with the ASEAN. An intelligent incentive structure needs to be framed. Industries also are discouraged from planning aggressive exports because of the high level of competitiveness in global markets. Therefore, it is essential to make the domestic industry competitive in world markets instead of giving them protection. Enhancing efficiency will help Industry to compete with China in the ASEAN market, and increase its export volumes.

8.4. POLICY IMPLICATIONS

In the light of the present study on India and ASEAN trade relations, of the following policy implications have been made for promoting viable trade partnership between the two.

1. India and the ASEAN need to build a partnership that can address two problems; i) challenges

associated with globalization, ii) close coordination to derive benefits of integration into the global economy. India and ASEAN can find many areas where they can cooperate, for example, in the areas of expansion of trade relation, security, and enhancing human resource capabilities.

2. India can play a crucial role with its growing economy and superiority in segments such as computer software, science & engineering for preserving peace and security in the region. India has acceded to "ASEAN's Treaty of Amity and Cooperation" during 2003 and has taken interest to work towards stabilizing the security and peace in the region. India also became a member of "ASEAN Regional Forum" that works in the areas of piracy, security and stability of the region by familiarizing the members about the various measures that it undertakes to promote its objectives.
3. India and the ASEAN, being part of ARF and other international initiatives, can utilize the opportunities to address concerns such as piracy of ships, drug trafficking, smuggling of arms and illegal transportation of humans.
4. Also, these nations could cooperate among themselves to assist and strengthen the United Nations to enable it to guard the international laws and give protection to weaker countries.
5. As global competition increases, it is necessary to continue with a positive outlook in the knowledge-based globalized economy. India and the ASEAN "should work closely under the Framework Agreement on Comprehensive Economic Cooperation to realize their economic potentials in trade in goods and services and investment as

soon as possible" (asean.org). These countries can enhance their competitiveness and can become a destination for goods and services in the global economy.

6. India and the ASEAN could also cooperate with other developing countries under the auspices of the World Trade Organization to ensure greater equity in global trade and that the globalization benefits all the countries. The countries should devise processes in such a way that the trade is not manipulated by a few countries or by some large MNCs.
7. India and the ASEAN can also take up the transport infrastructure to help trade promotion, tourism and other economic activities. Energy security is another area of common concern for both nations. They could look into promoting sustainable and optimal utilization of energy and alternative source of energy. Also, both sides should consider measures to enhance trade and investment in the energy sector.
8. India and ASEAN could cooperate in the areas of human resource development to build skills in people by learning from experiences of each other, and by exchanging information on the sectors where they enjoy a comparative advantage.
9. Also, India and the ASEAN could work in the area of cultural exchange and engage their people to interact among each other, especially among business, bureaucratic and academic communities so that there will be an increase in people's participation in the development programs. It will also promote reducing the differences in popular perceptions about each other countries.

10. India and the ASEAN, while working towards greater cooperation, also need to be aware of certain temporary instances which might strain the relations. Continuous engagement with frequent interactions and open communication channels are the key to avoid any such misunderstandings and continue the good relations: bureaucratic hurdles, red tape to be avoided in order to stimulate such healthy interactions.

8.5 CONCLUSION

There are many opportunities as well as challenges in front of India and ASEAN engagement. The partnership is an ongoing process, and it is unfolding. ASEAN and India should invest in nurturing the partnership so that it can become stronger despite the challenges posed by the globalization of world economies as well as several other issues. From time to time, new thrust to be given by respective governments and institutions to expand the scope of cooperation. ASEAN and India could work together to bring peace and prosperity to the region, which is being wished by all.

Bibliography

Books

1. Agarwal, M. R. (1979), "Regional Economic Cooperation in South Asia", Sultan Chand & Co. Ltd, New Delhi.
2. Aikman, David (1986), "Pacific Rim: Area of Change, Area of Opportunities", Little Brown & Co., Boston
3. Alessandrini, M., Fattouh B., Ferrarini B. & Scaramozzino, P. (2011), Tariff liberalization and Trade Specialization: Lessons from India, Journal of Comparative Economics, 39 (4): 499–513. Asian Development Bank, (1997), "Emerging Asia", ADB Publication.
4. Balassa, Bela;(1965), Trade Liberalisation and Revealed Comparative Advantage, *The Manchester School of Economic and Social Studies*, No. 33
5. Berger, Mark. T and Bora, Douglas A (ed) (1997), "The Rise of East Asia", Routledge, NY.
6. Bradford, Colin (ed) (1987), "Trade and Structural Change in Pacific Asia", UCP, Chicago.
7. Brown A. J., (1947) Applied Economics, Aspects of the World Economy in War and Peace. London,

8. Bugamelli, M. (2001), "Il Modello di Specializzazione Internazionale dell'Area Dell'euro e dei Principali Paesi Europei: Omogeneità e Convergenza. Temi di Discussione 402, Banca d'Italia, Rome (International Specialization Patterns of the Euro Area and the Main European Countries)." Discussion Paper No. 402. Rome: Italian Central Bank
9. Chen, Edward K.Y and Drysdale, Peter, (ed) (1995), "Corporate Links and FDI in Asia and the Pacific", Center for Asian Studies, Hongkong.
10. Cronin, Richard P. (1992), " Japan the United States, and Prospects for the Asia-Pacific Century: three scenarios for the future", St. Martin's Press, N.Y.
11. Curlis, Gerald. L. (ed), (1996), "The United States, Japan and Asia: Challenge for US Policy", Routledge, New York.
12. Dangler, Chuck (1993), 'The Pacific Rim Region: A World Market Place Approach through Trade and Investment", Madison Books, U.S.A.
13. Das, Dilip. K. (1996), "The Asia-Pacific Economy", MacMillan Press Ltd., N D.
14. Delhaise, Philippe K. (1998), "Asia in Crises", Wiley Publications, N.D.
15. Deng, Yong (1997), "Promoting Asia-Pacific Economic Cooperation: Perspectives from East Asia", MacMillan Press Ltd.
16. Deyo, Frederick (1987), "The Political Economy of the New Asian Industrialism", Pergamon Press, London.
17. Dirlik, Arif, (1986), " What's in a Rim: Critical Perspectives", Westview Press, New York.
18. Dobbs, Michael.S. Higginson (1993), "Asia-Pacific: A View on its Role in the' New World Order", Viking, Penguin Books, India, New Delhi.
19. Dr. Radha Raghuramapatruni; (2012) India's Trade with the ASEAN, ISBN 978-93-81136-51-5

20. Drysdale, Peter (1988), "International Economic Pluralism: Policy in East Asia and the Pacific", Alien and Unwin, Sydney.

21. Dzever, Sam arid Jaussaud, Jacques, (ed), (1997), "Perspectives on Economic integration and Business Strategy in the Asia-Pacific Region", Macmillan Press Ltd, London.

22. Edgardo, Campos Jose and Hilton, Root (1988), "The Key to the Asian Miracle: making shared growth credible", Brookings Institution, Washington.

23. Eiteljörge, U. and M. Hartmann (1999): Central-Eastern Europe Food Chains Competitiveness. Chapter 12 in The European Agro-Food System and the Challenge of Global Competition (ISMEA: Rome)

24. ESCAP, (1992), "Empirical Studies on Trade and Investment within the Asia-Pacific Region", ESCAP, UN.

25. ESCAP, (1992), "Expansion of Trade and Investment among ESCAP Developing Countries within a Regional Framework", ESCAP, UN.

26. ESCAP, (1996), "Asia and Pacific Developing Economies and the first Ministerial Conference: Issues of Concerns", ESCAP, U N.

27. Frank, Andre Gunder (1998), "Reorient Global Economy in the Asian Age", Vistas Publications, New Delhi.

28. Frankel, J. A, (1999), "Regional Trading Blocs in the World Economic System", Institute of International Economics, Washington D C.

29. Frederic Grare, Amitabh Mattoo, (2003); "Beyond the Rhetoric the Economies of India's Look East policy", Vol.I, Manohar Publishers, New Delhi.

30. Gamble, Andrew and Paynes, Anthony (ed) (1996), "Regionalism and World Order", MacMillan Press Ltd., London.

31. Garnaut, Ross (1994), "Asian Market, Economies: Challenges of a Changing International Environment", Institute of Southeast Asian Studies, Singapore.

32. Garnaut, Ross, Drysdale, Peter and Kunkel, John (ed) (1994), " Asia Pacific Regionalism: Readings in International Economic Relations", Harper Collins, NSW.

33. Gousal, B (1998), "ASEAN and South Asia: Development Experience", Sterling, N. D.

34. Green, Carl J. and Brewer, Thomas L. (ed), "Investment Issues in Asia and The Pacific", Oceana, N. Y.

35. Grubel, H., & Lloyd, P. (1975). Intra-industry trade: Theory and measurement of international trade in differentiated products. London: Macmillan.

36. Guglielmo Maria Caporale, Anamaria Sova and Robert Sova; (2015), Trade Flows and Trade Specialisation: The Case of China, DIW Berlin, German Institute for Economic Research, ISSN electronic edition 1619-4535, p 6

37. Hendrik Van den Berg, Joshua J. Lewer, M.E. Sharpe; (2007), International Trade and Economic Growth

38. Hertel, Thomas W. (ed) (1997), "Global Trade Analysis: Modeling and Applications", CUP.

39. Hoekman, Bernard and Djankov Simeon, (1997), "Determinants of the Export Structure of Countries in Central and Eastern Europe", World Bank Economic Review, 1997, Vol.11, issue 3, 471-87

40. Hsuing, James C. (ed) (1994), "Asia Pacific in the New World Politics", Lynnne Rienner Publishers, Boulder and London.

41. IIFT, (1995), "Studies in Trade and Investment: Review and Analysis of Intra regional Trade flows in Asia and the Pacific", IIFT, New Delhi.

42. Islam, Iyanatul and Chowdhury, Anis (1993), "The NIEs of East Asia", q, Routledge, London.

43. Islam, Iyanatul and Chowdhury, Anis (1997), "Asia-Pacific Economies: A Survey", Routledge London and N.Y.

44. J.F. Mejia; (2011), Export Diversification and Economic Growth, Contributions to Economics, DOI 10.1007/978-3-7908-2742-2_2, # Springer-Verlag Berlin Heidelberg

45. Jain, O. P (1993), "Regional Cooperation. for Trade in Asia: Export Opportunities for Indian", Delhi Commercial Publication Bureau, Delhi.

46. John Wong, (1979); "ASEAN Economies in Perspective – A comparative study of Indonesia, Malaysia, The Philippines, Singapore and Thailand", The Macmillan Press Limited, Hongkong.

47. Kiichiro, Fukasaku (ed) (1995), "Regional Cooperation and Integration in Asia", ADB.

48. Kris Olds, Peter; Dickens, Philip. F; Kelly, Lily Kong and Hunny, Wai-Chung Yeung (ed) (1999), "Globalisation and Asia-Pacific: Contested Territories", Routledge, NY.

49. Lafay, G. (1992), The Measurement of Revealed Comparative Advantage , in M. G. Dagenais and P. A. Muet, eds., International Trade Modelling, London, Chapman & Hall

50. Lasserre, (1994), "Strategies for Asia Pacific", MacMillan Press Ltd, London.

51. Lawrence, Robert. Z, (1996), "Regionalism, Multilateralism and Integration!', The Brooking Institution, Washington, DC.

52. Leamer, E.E, (1982), " Sources of International Comparative Advantage: Theory and Evidence", Cambridge, Mass, MIT Press.

53. Linnerman, H. (1966). "An Econometric study of world trade flows". Amsterdam Publishing House, Holland

54. Lo, Fu Chen and Akrasanee Narongchai (ed) (1992), 'The Future of Asia Pacific Economies": Emerging Role of Asian NICs and ASEAN", APDC, Allied Publishers.

55. Lo, Fu Chen and Salih, Kamal (ed) (1987), "The Challenge of Asia Pacific Cooperation", ADIPA, Malaysia.

56. Mack, Andrew and Ravenhill, John (ed) (1995), "Pacific Cooperation: Building Economic and Security Regimes in the Asia Pacific Region", Westview Press, Colombia.

57. McGrew, Anthony and Brook, Christopher (ed) (1998), "Asia-Pacific in the New World Order", Routledge, New York.

58. Naisbitt, John and Aburdeen, Patricia (1991), "Megatrends 2000", Nicholas, Brealey, London.

59. Naisbitt, John, (1994), "Global Paradox", First Avon Books, N.Y.

60. Naisbitt; John (1995), "Megatrends- Asia ", Avon Books, N Y.

61. Narendra Prasad (2004); "India's International Trade and Economic Reforms", Kanishka publishers Distributors, New Delhi.

62. Nemetz, Peter N. (ed) (1987), "The Pacific Rim Investment, Development and Trade", University of British Columbia Press, Vancouver.

63. Nguyen, D. T. and Roy, K.C (1994), "Economic Reforms, Liberalization and Trade in the Asia Pacific Region", Wiley Eastern Ltd, N.D.

64. Palmer, Norman (1991), 'The New Regionalism in Asia and the Pacific", Mass Lexington Books.

65. Panchamukhi V. R - (1989), "Growth Trade and Structural Change in the Asian Region", RIS, New Delhi.

66. Panchamukhi V. R (1987), "Planning, Development and the World Economic Order", Radiant Publishers, New Delhi.

67. Panchamukhi V. Rand Sobhan, Rehman. (ed) (1995), "Towards an Asian. Economic Area", RIS, New Delhi.

68. Paul Krugman and Maurice Obstfeld; (2006), International Economics: Theory and Policy, 7th Edition

69. Quibria, M. G (ed) (1995), "Critical Issues in Asian Development: Theories, Experiences and Policies", 0smania University Press.

70. Radke, Kurt. W; Stam, Joop. A; Groenwegen, John; Van de May, Leo. M; Akiyama, Takuo (ed) (1998), "Dynamics in Pacific Asia: Conflict, Competition and Cooperation'" Kyan Paul International, London and N.Y.

71. Ramu, Shiva (1996), "The Dragons of Asia: Asia Pacific Rim Countries and their Multinationals", India.

72. Rohwer, Jim (1995), "Asia Rising: How history's Biggest middle class will change the world", Butter worth - Heinemann Asia.

73. Russet, Bruce. M (1996), " The Asia Rim land as a Region for containing China", The Asian Society, N.Y.

74. Satyanarayan, B, (1986), "India's Trade with Asia and the Far East Countries", B.R Publishing Corp, New Delhi.

75. Shaw, Timothy. M (ed) (1995), "Economic Restructuring in East Asia and India", International Political Economy Series.

76. Sindhwani, 1. N (1975) "Economic Feasibility of an Asian Common Market", Sterling Publishers Pvt Ltd, New Delhi.

77. Singh, Romani. K. Kumar (1976), "India's Trade with South East Asia", Chugh Publications, Allahabad, India.

78. Steven M. Suronovic: (2010), International Trade: Theory and Policy, Flat World Knowledge Inc., ISBN-10: 1936126443, ISBN-13: 978-1936126446

79. Streeton, Paul (ed) (1988), "Beyond Adjustment: The Asian Experience", IMF Publication.

80. Stubbs, Richard and Underhill, Geoffrey R .0 (ed) (1991) "Political Economy and the Changing Global Order", The Macmillan Press Ltd, UK.

81. Tan, Joseph L. H (ed) (1930), " Regional Economic Cooperation in the Asia Pacific" Stanford Press Ltd, Singapore.

82. Thomas, Vinod and Stephens, Peter (1994), "The East Asian Miracle", World Bank Publication, Washington, 0 C.

83. Tipton, Frank B. (1998), "The Rise of Asia", Macmillan Press Ltd, UK.

84. Vashisht, Prem (ed): (1989), "Commonalities, Complementarities and Cooperation: Asia-Pacific Region", ADIPA, 1989.

85. World Bank (1998), "The Road to Recovery", A WB Publication.

86. Yu, George T. (ed) (1997), 'Asia's New World Order", MacMillan Press Ltd.

Articles and Research Papers:

1. Alag, Yoginder K, "India and Regional Development Cooperation", Paper presented at International Conference on Asia-Pacific and the Global Order, Oct 2-4, 2000.

2. Alessandrini, Michele; Fattouh Bassam; Ferrarini Benno; Scaramozzino, Pasquale;(December 2011) "Tariff Liberalization and trade specialization : Lessons from India", Journal of Comparative Economics, Vol.39, Issue 4

3. ALLEYNE, Antonio1, LORDE, Troy (2014), A Gravity Model Approach to The Trade Performance of

CARICOM member states, Applied Econometrics and International Development, Vol. 14-2

4. Ambatkar, Sanjay, "Modalities for Convergence of Economic Interests between India and ASEAN", Indian Ocean Digest, Jan-Jun 2000.
5. Ambatkar, Sanjay, "Trends in Foreign Investment Interaction between India and ASEAN in the 1990s", Paradigm, Vol 5, No: 1,2001.
6. Anderson, Kim, "Is an Asia-Pacific trade Bloc Next", Journal *of* World Trade, August 1991.
7. Asher, Mukul G; Sen, Rahul and Srivastava, Sadhana, "ASEAN-India: Emerging Opportunities", Paper presented at ASEAN-India Workshop, March 17-18,2001.
8. Atul Sarma, Pradeep Kumar Mehta, "ASEAN as A Regional Bloc", Foreign Trade Review, 2016
9. Bagchi, A, "Growth Miracle and its unravelling in East and South East Asia", EPW, Vol 33, No: 18,1998.
10. Baru, Sanjay, "India and ASEAN: The Emerging Economic Relationship towards a Bay of Bengal Community", Paper presented at IOSC, O.U, Feb 11-13,1999.
11. Bergstrand, Jeffrey H., (1985), "The Gravity equation in International Trade: Some Micro Economic Foundations and Empirical Evidence", The Review of Economics and Statistics, Vol.67, No..3 pp 474-481
12. Bohdan Vahalík; (March 2014), Regional Bilateral Trade Analysis of the European Union, China and ASEAN, Enterprise and the Competitive Environment 2014 conference, ECE 2014, Brno, Czech Republic, ScienceDirect, Procedia Economics and Finance 12 (2014) 709 – 717
13. Brada, J. C., & Mendez, J. (1983). Regional economic integration and the volume of intra-regional trade: a comparison of developed and developing country experience. *Kyklos*, *36*(4), 589-603

14. Business Week, "The New World's Newest Trading Bloc", B.W, May 4, 1992.
15. C Nalin Kumar; (2009), ASEAN India FTA and commodity trade: prioritising invisible infrastructure, Indian Institute of Plantation Management, Jnana Bharathi Campus, Bangalore – 560 056. Email: nalin.kumar1@gmail.com
16. Constantine Michalopoulos Francis Ng; (May 2013) Developing Country Trade Policies and Market Access Issues, 1990–2012, The World Bank, Development Research Group, Trade and Integration Team, WPS6463 Public
17. Daniel Jacobius Morgan; (2012), From China to ASEAN: Rebalancing India's trade, Gateway House, Indian Council on Global Relations, 14th Dec 2012
18. Dharmarajan, K and Bhattacharya, B, "Regional Integration through Trade and Investment, Asia Pacific Development Monitor, Vol1, No: 11,1999.
19. Dirlik, Arif, "The Asia-Pacific Idea: Reality and Representation in the Invention of a Regional Structure", Journal *of* World History, 3, No: 1, 1992.
20. Dr. Pradeep Kumar; (2012), INDIA, CHINA AND ASEAN, ACADEMICIA: An International Multidisciplinary Research journal, Published by South Asian Academic Research Journals, Vol 2, Issue 4, ISSN 2249-7137
21. East Asian Economies: The Crises of 1997-98", EPW, 33(23), 1998.
22. Eastern Economist, 1979, "Economic Cooperation with ASEAN", Vol 72, (18).
23. Eleck, Andrew, "APEC: Motives, Objectives, Prospects", Australian Journal of International Affairs, 46, 2, 1992.
24. Etienne, Gilbert, "From Miracles to Mirages", Business, Jan 9, 1998.

25. Gokarn, Subir, "More lessons from East Asia", Business Standard, Feb 9, 1998.
26. Gokarri, Subir, "The East Asian Crises of 1997: Some Implications for India", India Development Report, *2000*.
27. Goldar, B. N, and Etsuro, Ishigani, "FDI in Asia", EPW, May 29,1999.
28. Greenspan, Alan "The Anatomy of the Crises and "The Weakest Links in the Chain", Economic Times, Dec 8 & 9,1997.
29. Habibullah, K, "Development Planning in ASEAN: Lessons of Experience", Economic Bulletin for Asia and the Pacific, 1998.
30. Higgots, Richards, "Asia-Pacific Economic Cooperation: Theoretical Opportunities and Practical Constraints", The Pacific Review, 6, 2, 1993.
31. Janardhan N, "Changing Perspectives of Asia and the Pacific", IASSI Quarterly, 1989.
32. Jitendra Kumar Badjatya, Ramesh Bodla, Pankaj Musyuni; (2013), EXPORT REGISTRATION OF PHARMACEUTICALS IN REST OF WORLD COUNTRIES (ROW), Journal of Drug Delivery & Therapeutics; 3(1), 61-64
33. Jomq, K S, "Tigers in Trouble: Financial Governance, Liberalisation and Crises in East Asia", Asia-Pacific Development Journal, Vol 5, No: 2, Dec 1998.
34. Juan Wang, Yusheng Kong, Haijun Wang; (February 2013), Analysis of China's Import from & Direct Investment in ASEAN—Based on Gravity Models, Technology and Investment, 4, 13-21, Scientific Research, (http://www.scirp.org/journal/ti)
35. Keya Chaturvedi: (May 2014) Deepening India's export Basket, NUS, East Asia Forum
36. Kurth, James, "The Pacific Basin versus the Atlantic Alliance: Two Paradigms of International Relations",

Annals of American Academy *of* Political and Social Sciences, Sept. 1989.

37. Meenu Tiwari, C. Veeramani, Manjeeta Singh; (January 2015), The potential for involving India in regional production networks: Analyzing vertically specialised trade patterns between India and ASEAN, Working Paper 292, Indian Council for research on International Economic relations

38. Ministry of Commerce & Industry Department of Commerce; Mid-Term Review of "Strategy for Doubling Exports in three years (2011-12 to 2013-14)". (Economic Division), Draft Discussion Paper

39. Mitsuyo Ando; (August 2006), Fragmentation and Vertical Intra-Industry trade in East Asia, Science Direct, North American Journal of Economics and Finance

40. Mohammed Saqib and Nisha Taneja; (July 2005), Non-Tariff Barriers and India's Exports: The case of ASEAN and Sri Lanka, Working Paper No.165, Indian Council for Research on International Economic Relations

41. Montagon, Peter, "Asia's Endangered Tigers", Financial Times, Dec 5, 1997.

42. Montreevat, Sakulrat, "Lessons from the Asian Crises: A Southeast Asian Perspective" ASEAN-India Workshop March 17-18, 2001.

43. Nassir Ul Haq Wani, Jaideep Kaur Dhami,(February, 2013) " Indo-China Trade : Intensity and Potential for Future Trade", International Journal of Enhanced Research in Educational Development, Vol. 1, Issue 1.

44. Nasrudin, Bonar M. Sinaga, Muhammad Firdaus, Dedi Walujadi; (May-June 2014), China-ASEAN Free Trade: Complementary or Competition, IOSR Journal of Economics and Finance (IOSR-JEF), e-ISSN: 2321-5933, p-ISSN: 2321-5925.Volume 3, Issue 4. pp. 23-31, www.iosrjournals.org

45. Niru Yadav; (January 2010), India Asian FTA A move towards Multilateral Free Trade Agreements? Briefing Paper, CUTS centre for International Trade, Economics & Environment

46. Oguledo V.I., MacPhee C.R. (1994), Gravity Models: a reformulation and an application to discriminatory trade arrangements, Applied Economics, 26, 107- 120

47. Patel, Surendra J, "East Asia's Spectacular Development: It's Lessons for Others", Asia Pacific Development Journal, Vol1, No: 1, June 1994.

48. Prema-chandra Athukorala; (August 2010), Production Networks and Trade Patterns in East Asia: Regionalisation or Globalisation? ADB working paper series on Regional Economic Integration, No.56, Asian Development Bank

49. Radhika Kak; (August 2014), India – Unleashing the ASEAN opportunity, Otg (On the ground), Global Research, Standard Chartered Bank India. Radhika.Kak@sc.com

50. Rajan Sudesh Ratna, Murali Kallumma; (2013), ASEAN–India Free Trade Agreement (FTA) and its Impact on India: A Case Study of Fisheries and Selected Agricultural Products, Foreign Trade Review, 48, 4: Indian Institute of Foreign Trade, SAGE Publications p 481–497

51. Rao, Bhanoji V. V, "East Asian Economies: Growth within an International Context", EPW, 33(6), 1998a.

52. Rao, Bhanoji V. V, "The East Asian Crises of 1997-98: Implications for Indja" Global Business Review, Voll, Jan-Jun 2000.

53. Reddy, Mehender J, "FDI in Malaysia: Opportunities and Lessons for India", Paper presented at Seminar on India-Malaysia Relations since 1990, Institute of Asian Studies, Hyderabad, Dec 22-23, 2001.

54. Sabyasachi Tripathi and Nuno Carlos Leitao (March 2013), India's Trade and Gravity Model: A Static and Dynamic panel Data, Institute of Social and

Economic Change, Polytechnic Institute of Satar_em, CEFAGE, University of Evora, MPRA Paper No.45502

55. Saman, Kelegama, "Open Regionalism and APEC", EPW, Vol 35, No: 51, Dec 16, 2000.
56. Sapir, Andre; Lutz, Ernst, (1981) Trade in services: economic determinants and development related issues (English). Staff working paper; no. SWP 480. Washington, D.C.: The World Bank.
57. Sarath Chandran, B.P.(2018), "Trade Impact of the India-ASEAN Free Trade Agreement (FTA): An Augmented Gravity Model Analysis" , MPRA Paper No. 84183
58. Sarma, Atul and Mehta, Pradeep Kumar, "Indo-ASEAN Trade Prospects: A Study of Trade Complementarity", ASEAN-India Workshop, March 17-18, 2001.
59. Shankaran Nambiar; (August 2011), India's Engagement with ASEAN: Beyond Trade in Goods, ISAS Working Paper, No.129, Institute of South Asian Studies, National University of Singapore
60. Shetty K. and Prasad S.B, "Comparative Advantage Theory and American Investment in Developing Nations", Foreign Trade Review, 1973,7(4).
61. Singh, Manmohan, "Globalisation and the Asia-Pacific Region: Challenges and Opportunities", Asia-Pacific Development Journal, Vol 4, No: 2, Dec 1997.
62. Sivakumar, S, "China and India: A Comparison", Business Standard, Dec 31, 2001.
63. Smitha Francis; (January 2011), A Sectoral Impact Analysis of the ASEAN-India Free Trade Agreement, Vol XLVI No.2, Economic & Political Weekly
64. Stubbs, Richards, "Geopolitical and Political Economy of South East Asia", International Journal, Vol44, 1988.
65. Sumann Choudary (2006); "A Study of India's political and Economic cooperation with ASEAN

countries", Abstract of Ph.D Thesis, Dept of Political Science, Jamia Millia Islamia, New Delhi.

66. Suthiphand Chirathivat & Anupama Masali; (August 2012), Building Connectivity for Deepening ASEAN-India Economic Integration, ASEAN-India strategic partnership: perspectives from ASEAN-India network of Think-Tanks, Proceedings of the First Round Table on ASEAN-India Network of Think-Tanks, p 42

67. The Asian Wall Street Journal, "Asia New World Order Strut", AWSJ, May 25, 1993. Perkins, D.H, ''There are at least three Models *of* East Asian Development", World Development, Vo122, No: 4,1994.

68. The Asian Wall Street Journal, "Asian Economic Growth may change World Order", AWSJ, May 17, 1992.

69. The Star, "PM: Asia will be Home to Economic Miracles", The Star, May1, 1993.

70. Tulas Tambunan (2006); "Is still ASEAN relevant in the era of the ASEAN-China FTA? Asia-Pacific Economic Association (APEA), Seattle, USA, July 29th-30th.

71. UNIDO Report, "Industrialisation in Asia and the Pacific Region, Principles and Programmes of Action", Vienna, UNIDO, 1974.

72. USITC Publication 4176; (Aug 2010) ASEAN: Regional Trends in Economic Integration, Export Competitiveness, and Inbound Investment for Selected Industries, Investigation No. 332-551, United States International Trade Commission. pages 6 -1 to 6 - 15

73. Vinayak HV, Fraser Thompson, Oliver Tonby; (May 2014), Understanding ASEAN: Seven things that you need to know, McKinsey& Co, Article, Insights & Publications

74. Volrath, T.L;(1991), A Theoretical Evaluation of Alternative TradeIntensity Measures of Revealed

Comparative Advantage, *Weltwirtschaftliches Archiv*, 130,265-279

75. Witada Anukoonwattaka and Mia Mikic; (2011), India: A new player in ASEAN production networks? In collaboration with the ASIA PACIFIC RESEARCH AND TRAINING NETWORK ON TRADE, Studies in Trade & Investment 75, Economic and Social Commission for Asia and Pacific, an UN Publication
76. Wood, Adrain and Calandrino, "When the Other Giant Awakens: Trade and Human Resources in India", EPW, Vol: 35, No: 52 & 53, Dec 30, 2000.
77. Yu Sheng, Hsiao Chink Tang, and Xinpeng Xu; (July 2012), The Impact of ACFTA on People's Republic of China–ASEAN Trade: Estimates Based on an Extended Gravity Model for Component Trade, ADB Working Paper Series on Regional Economic Integration, No.99, Asian Development Bank
78. Yumiko Okamoto, (2005); "China-India; Challenges and Opportunities for ASEAN from Japanese Perspectives", Dept of Policy Studies, Doshisha university, Kyoto, Japan.
79. Yung Chul Park, "Globalisation and Regional Integration in Pacific Asia", ESCAP, Development Planning Division, 1992.
80. Zhao Hong, (2006); "China's perspective on India's changing relations with ASEAN" ICS Working Paper Series No. 20012, Malaysia.

Reports and Documents:

1. AINTT (ASEAN-India Network of Think Tanks) Round Table proceedings
2. International Financial Statistics, IMF.
3. Direction of Trade Statistics, IMF.
4. Balance of Payments Statistics, IMF.
5. Statistical Yearbook, UN.

6. Foreign Trade Statistics Yearbook, UN.
7. Statistical Yearbook for Asia and the Pacific, ESCAP, UN.
8. Statistical Indicators for Asia and the Pacific, ESCAP, UN.
9. Foreign Trade Statistics for Asia and the Pacific, ESCAP, UN.
10. Economic and Social Survey for Asia and the Pacific, ESCAP, UN.
11. World Investment Report, UNCTAD, UN. I
12. World Investment Directory, UNCTAD, UN.
13. Human Development Report, UNDP, UN.
14. World Development Report, World Bank.
15. World Development. Indicators World Bank.
16. World Economic and Social Survey, World Bank.
17. Asian Development Outlook, Asian Development Bank.
18. Key Indicators for Developing Asia and the Pacific, Asian Development Bank.
19. Economic Survey, Government of India.
20. Reserve Bank of India, Bulletins, RBI.
21. Indian Planning Experience: A Statistical Profile, Planning Commission, Government of India.
22. UNCTAD Commodity Yearbook, UN & New York.
23. UNCTAD Commodity Handbook of Statistics, UN & New York.

List of Working Paper Series

1. Reserve Bank of India (RBI) Occasional Papers.
2. Centre for Strategic and International Studies (CSIS) Working Paper Series.
3. Indian Council for Research on International Economic Relations (ICRIER)

4. The Centre for International Governance Innovation Working Papers.
5. Institute of Policy Studies (IPS) Working Papers.
6. Institute of Chinese Studies (ICS) Working Papers.
7. Institute of South Asian Studies (ISAS) Working Papers.
8. Research and Information System for Developing Countries (RIS) Working Papers.
9. Asian Development Bank (ADB).

List of Websites:

www.rbi.org.in

www.unctad.org

www.asean.org

www.asean.co.id

www.asean-india.org

www.adb.org

www.icrier.org

www.economist.com/countries

www.iseas.edu.sg

www.unescap.org

www.globalpolicy.org

www.washingtontimes.com

www.thehindubusinessline.com

www.bbc.com

www.csis.org